UNFOCUSED

UNFOCUSED

THE JOURNEY TO SELF-ACTUALIZATION

ESTER TEPER

NEW DEGREE PRESS
COPYRIGHT © 2021 ESTER TEPER
All rights reserved.

UNFOCUSED
The Journey to Self-Actualization

ISBN	978-1-63730-682-6	*Paperback*
	978-1-63730-771-7	*Kindle Ebook*
	979-8-88504-035-8	*Ebook*

To my mom, who fostered both my drive and my laziness, and Deda, who shows the world what "killing with kindness" truly means.

To my mentors, who have come in the form of friends, family, teachers, and role models, without whom none of my success would be possible.

CONTENTS

INTRODUCTION	11
HOW DO I READ THIS BOOK?	19
DEFINING SELF-ACTUALIZATION	21

PART I. GENEROSITY — 41
- GRATITUDE — 47
- APPRECIATION THROUGH ACTION — 61
- UNDERSTANDING — 75
- TL;DR — 91

PART II. COURAGE — 93
- TAKE RISKS — 95
- NEVER ASSUME — 115
- EXPLORE WITHOUT LIMITS — 133
- TL;DR — 147

PART III. AUTHENTICITY — 149
- PURPOSEFUL THINKING IN AVOIDING GOAL-RELIANCE — 155
- THINK BIG AND IDENTIFY YOUR TRUE "WHY" — 175
- VISUALIZE YOUR "WHY" IN ACTION — 199
- ALIGN YOUR "HOW" TO CREATE SYNERGY — 217
- TL; DR — 233

CONCLUSION	235
ACKNOWLEDGMENTS	239
APPENDIX	243

Life is a journey, not a destination.

Happiness is not "there" but here, not "tomorrow" but today.

—RABBI SIDNEY GREENBERG

INTRODUCTION

Success. What does it look like to you? Is it money? Fame? Legacy? Maybe it's love, human connection, philanthropy? Don't think about it in terms of what's possible or impossible by your current standards and limitations; think about what you want out of life. What does that look like? What have your family, friends, and mentors made it out to be? How has that changed over the last few months or years?

Determining what success means for the individual is *hard*. It is ever-changing, especially as you or I may achieve a goal we've been working toward for a while, or as the world around us changes. The influences of parents, teachers, media, and mentors make it difficult to differentiate between what you want and what the world wants for you.

For one person, success might mean waking up in the morning, rolling out of bed, putting on a cute dress, and heading to manage the business they founded. For another, it is attending a meditation retreat on the way to the mall for a styling gig. In either scenario, today has the opportunity to be a culmination of your efforts, filled with gratitude, new beginnings, and smiles...

That is why in this book, we will use a different term: *self-actualization*. We will define it ad nauseam, but for now, think about it as a chemical reaction: add a bit of success, a bit of fulfillment, and lots of hard work. It needs to be stirred constantly to keep the inertia of the reaction moving forward, and it can only work under the right conditions. In the lab, those would be temperature and pressure; in your life, they will be your values and your mission.

Self Actualization: Success + Fulfillment + Hard work

So now take a moment and think about that special ending you contemplated above. What comes after? How will you spend your days? What, if anything, will change? If your ideal ending is *becoming* president, what will you do once you achieve that role? What will define your tenure? If your ideal ending is a marriage, what happens after the wedding day? After you drive off to enjoy the honeymoon?

Self-actualization isn't just described by getting the ideal ending, but also by living the ideal life following it.

Self-actualization is about understanding there is more than a career. In the process of writing this book, I found I would not be able to define and explore self-actualization alone, so I turned to conducting interviews, starting off with people I knew, and then branching out around the world. I asked each person to note a few inflection points or memorable moments in life that created some shift in life course. Many initially processed the question with a sentiment of goal-orientation, pointing to notable times in their professional careers, but would then pivot while thinking out loud. "On second thought, that doesn't define my life... My life is defined by my family, by my happiness, and the way I feel about the world," said Darryl Berger, a highly successful New Orleans real estate developer.

That is why my future life is filled with the word "comfort" and everything it brings. Comfort in knowing I had an accomplished career and made enough money to fulfill all my needs. Comfort in having a life partner I can rely on day to day, but also have them challenge me continuously and push me to be better. Comfort in the legacy I will leave behind: hopefully one of a joyful, carefree person who loves life. These are all elements of my fairytale, but also long-term commitments to personal growth that don't just end when I make a million dollars, marry, start a business, or have children. Comfort in life is all about continuous progress, through learning and interaction.

For me, this has been quite difficult. Ever since I was five years old, I had the goal of getting into an Ivy League institution presented to me by my parents. In elementary school, bratty little Ester would annoy all her teachers about any small mistakes on tests to make sure she had the highest earned grade possible. Extra credit was her best friend. Middle school Ester worked with her science teacher to design experiments for external competitions, and although she didn't win, she was still really proud of herself. High school Ester got involved in and led every club possible, whether it be the Math and Chess Club, the school musical, the newspaper, or scientific research.

I lived with blinders on, seeing only this one guideline of getting into an Ivy League university as the compass for my life. The expectations were clear: earn good grades, get excellent teacher recommendations, stand out through extracurriculars, and make valuable connections with admissions officers. So, mini-Ester went through school with this one goal always at the back of her head.

Upon being accepted to top-tier universities, but unfortunately not any Ivy League universities, I found myself lost. I had been working toward this goal for the past thirteen years of my life with nothing else in mind but school, academic excellence, and standing out for the eight top-tier admission committees I had my heart set on to impress. I found myself lacking purpose, but also not completely understanding why I was even involved in the organizations I was in charge of. I had become a victim of *goal-reliance*, my new term for being addicted to the goals presented to me by family, friends, peers, and mentors, rather than truly looking within myself and understanding what I was interested in.

Yet, I went into college with the same mentality: graduate with a wonderful engineering degree and a 4.00, go to a combined JD-PhD program for graduate school, and then be employed by the pharmaceutical industry for my expertise in biomedical engineering and patent law. Sounds impressive, right? I thought so, too.

Then I took my first college-level biology class and decided biomedical engineering wasn't for me. I enrolled myself in three lab sciences and recognized I simply could never complete a PhD in biology or engineering because that would require spending around five years in gloves and other personal protective equipment. This wouldn't work, so I shifted my path ever so slightly to chemical engineering and engineering management, allowing for flexibility and exploration of other interests. My electives became focused on management and communications. I stopped participating in organizations I was uninterested in or made me feel less than or unwanted. My vision began to align a bit more with my interests and abilities. Sometimes, a big change comes from something minimal.

Further, upon coming to college, for the first time in my life I found myself surrounded by a truly diverse group of people. It was *weird*. I constantly felt like I was going to say the wrong thing and offend someone with my words unintentionally. Students came from high and low socioeconomic status (SES), different racial and cultural backgrounds, and thousands of unique stories. It soon became a personal challenge: getting to understand the backgrounds of the people around me. One thing that stuck out to me from particular individuals were their histories, present stories, and future aspirations. I found these individuals had very strong value bases. They had a defined hierarchy for their interactions, where they knew what was important to them, and they simply did not stray from it.

Being in this unique environment, and as I transitioned away from participating in things that did not serve any purpose in my life, I also began to care more about the people around me. I began to devote more time to the religious organizations on Vanderbilt's campus, volunteering several hours a week, and committing myself to self-improvement.

I realized I was lacking in core values. In my obsession with attaining admission to the top universities in the country, I had failed miserably at developing myself as a person. I did not know what I stood for, or what was important to me. There was no code I lived by, and I had no interests outside of the ones required for my college application.

I dove into the realm of positive psychology and buried myself in self-improvement books. These became a hallmark of my life, and as anyone who comes into my room would tell you, they are everywhere. "Could psychology be a part of my mission?" became a question the popped into my head quite frequently.

Reading had been something I had enjoyed but lost in my pursuit of an oddly specific goal that lacked meaning. Since then, I have made reading a key part of my routine, as it is an activity that improves my mental and emotional base, elevates me, and bring me closer to my self-actualized being. Activities like this might seem like a hassle, but once you start, you are engaged and thankful to be so. It's founded in cognitive dissonance, when you're so used to doing one thing that when you do another—even if it's right—your mind and body face a conflict. Examples for me have included reading, exploring new restaurants, traveling to new places, or taking classes outside of my core competencies. All technically "optional," but these passive activities improve my physical, mental, and emotional presence. We'll explore these in depth in the book.

Over the past few months, I have been thinking about and revising my personal belief system and constantly pushing myself toward living a more fulfilled life. An interesting statistic that sparked this process was that three out of every ten are satisfied with their job. My immediate response was, "What about the other seven?" (Pew Research Center, 2016). I hope this book serves as a guide toward fulfillment for those other seven still searching and hoping to reach their full potential. Through defining the entirety of your life as a fairytale, rather than putting a stop sign at particular points that could be fairytale endings, you don't set yourself up for disappointment when that ending does come.

In my interviews with CEOs, religious leaders, important government officials, and some of the happiest people I know, "What's next?" became a common question, especially when you have it "all." By not defining an end, everything is a possible next. Participating in activities that refresh you will keep you strong and motivated. Building your life based on your passions will create a new, and more real, you.

Thus, emerge the necessary steps to living a self-actualized life: having a core set of values, a defined mission, and a fluid and adjustable vision. All of these must be yours and yours alone. We will work through examples and possibilities, others' stories of successes and failures, so that you can grasp these concepts further. For now, remember that thought from the very beginning?

What does the future you, the reader, look like in your perfect world? Think about it.

HOW DO I READ THIS BOOK?

My little sister recently described her book-reading process. She looks at a book, decides if the cover is pretty, and only then embarks on the journey of reading the first page. Quickly, she becomes frustrated or bored, and quits.

By far, the worst experience you can have with any book is picking one up with a cover that speaks to you, reading the introduction or prologue and getting excited, and then starting the first chapter and being bored to death. So let me spare you.

This book is meant to shift your perspectives through others' stories and nudge you in the direction of an improved and more authentic self. The first chapter is one of definitions, heavily research based, and definitely the most difficult to read. I encourage you to take the time to go through it because, as we will soon learn, our brain tends to avoid difficulties. If you repeat complex tasks enough times, they become easy—our brains learn.

The rest of the book is split up into three parts: Generosity, Courage, and Authenticity. These are core values self-actualized individuals possess, and with each third, the push toward action increases. Each chapter will challenge you to think past your current existence and believe in a future that has more color, more light, and more joy. At the end of each part, you will find a "TL;DR," which stands for "Too Lazy; Didn't Read." It is a brief summary of the important points to make it easier to remember and share what you just read!

Good luck!

CHAPTER 1

DEFINING SELF-ACTUALIZATION

I work really hard at trying to see the big picture and not getting stuck in ego. I believe we're all put on this planet for a purpose, and we all have a different purpose... When you connect with that love and that compassion, that's when everything unfolds.

—ELLEN DEGENERES

In 2019, a twenty-seven-year-old Indian man came to the decision to sue his parents for bringing him into the world without his consent. He claimed it was not his decision to be born, and because this was done, he has to put up with lifelong suffering (Pandey, 2019).

According to Jewish traditions, though, each soul is brought to this earth for a reason: The world would not be complete without your unique contribution, your skills and talents, and your presence (Dubov). You are here because you are needed, and it is through the process of self-actualization you can become the best version of yourself. You begin to live instead of merely existing.

The journey to self-actualization is a deeply personal one, and when analyzing something this general, the importance of definitions cannot be minimized. There are multiple definitions in existence of the term self-actualization, all of which are valid, but we will be streamlining the one we use for the context of this book.

In short, *self-actualization is the ability to reach your full potential.* There will be three aspects to this definition:

1. Self-actualization is a constant process.
2. Self-actualization requires challenges and obstacles.
3. Self-actualization looks different for everyone, and only you can define it.

The concept of self-actualization is nothing new. Kurt Goldstein, a biologist, actually coined the term, and psychologist Carl Rogers then further expanded on it. The context in which you have heard about it likely varies, but it was through Abraham Maslow's hierarchy of psychological needs that the term made it into the vocabulary of the general population. In this book, we will use a combination of the three theorists' definitions (Britannica, 2019).

Kurt Goldstein's Biological Definition and the Origin of the Term Self-Actualization

Kurt Goldstein views self-actualization as a driving force that allows us to explore what is right or wrong, and what ultimately allows us to fulfill our potentialities. Potentialities, not potential. Why? Because potentialities refer to all the skills and talents you may have, rather than your single being. Goldstein, to whom this term can be attributed, explores the impact of environment on the individual in his book *The Organism*.

Specifically, he points out the environment an organism lives in is dynamic and constantly changing, and it is a direct result of the organism's development. Just as the organism itself influences its environment, its environment will be a key component of gene expression, activation, and regulation, all of which create not only the brain's architecture, but also the organism's personality and behavioral tendencies.

For Harold Daniel, former president of the Georgia State Bar, a change in environment influenced him to have a major inflection point in his life. He was at a bat mitzvah, which he had dreaded attending because of the rough week he had. In his world, everything revolved around the law, especially the corporate organizations he was working for at the time.

At the bat mitzvah, there was assigned seating, so Daniel ended up sitting between his wife and another relative who had come down from New Jersey to celebrate the occasion. As he got to know his neighbor, her recent trip to Africa came up, where she had climbed Mount Kilimanjaro. He looked at her, a woman around fifty years old, and told her he wished he had done this ten or twenty years ago, as he was now sixty-eight years old.

"You can," she responded. These were exactly the words he needed to hear. He set off on a research spiral, and less than a year later, found himself 19,347 miles in the air at the summit of Mt. Kilimanjaro. This was a change in perspective for Daniel, a moment of pure fulfillment, making him appreciate his health and ability to still make life-defining memories. Daniel achieving what he set his mind on allowed him to think in a new way and grow like he never thought he would.

On his climb down, he asked the guide, who had made the trip over one hundred times by that point, if he was the oldest person to successfully complete the climb. To his surprise, the guide laughed and said the oldest was actually eighty-three! Once again, in a different environment, he would have never been given the chance to learn about the possibilities and how his age is just a number, rather than a limitation. The development associated with self-actualization can occur at any point in life, and Daniel's experience is the perfect example of this.

In a high development stage, such as early childhood or the transition from puberty into adulthood, the brain's architecture is highly sensitive and our capabilities on a physical, mental, and emotional level have an opportunity to be improved upon (Fox, Levitt, and Nelson, 2010). With each new experience in a particular environment, the brain learns how to respond faster and better and becomes more effective at recognizing patterns. The more scenarios like that arise, the "better" the brain will function. In the example of learning how to play an instrument, whenever you learn how to play a new set of chords, the better your brain will get at it.

Due to this ability for constant improvement allowed for by the brain's elasticity, Goldstein was able to build his theory of self-actualization. He founded the theory on nature's tendency to shift toward disorder, as the second law of thermodynamics suggests. His logically drawn conclusion was an organism will be successful in finding the right environment if it finds and has order. This element of order comes from the actualization, or achievement of the full potential, of the being.

In a real-life example, think about the cycle of doing laundry. On the first day, you do your laundry, put everything away in its rightful place, and your living space is clean. Each day, you need to put on clothes, creating the possibility for a mess. There are now two options: putting in a little bit of energy consistently and maintaining the clean room, or allowing your room to become messier and messier, until it gets to a point where you need to put in a much larger amount of energy to return to its clean state.

In this example, the room is the environment, and the messy laundry is something impacting the environment. Cleaning is an energy expenditure. If doing laundry is something you enjoy, you will put in the effort each day to clean up after yourself, maintaining as much order as is possible, given the fact you have to wear clean clothing every day.

Simply put, we naturally find ourselves in a state of disorder, and self-actualization is the return to order where we then find ourselves more fulfilled. From a biological perspective, fulfillment means physical safety, easy acquisition of food and water, and the ability to reproduce successfully. A self-actualized individual knows how to handle these new scenarios by creating order, using the practiced and adapted brain.

To explain the instinctual needs of any living being, Goldstein breaks down the cognitive focus of the being on the need.

Let's break that down. There are two parts of life: the foreground and the background. The foreground is the organism's highest priority, but the background can be more of the way of life, such as the values of the individual. An organism that takes the background into account when coping with the foreground will be successful.

Think about it as the short-term goals that exist in your life and the long-term ones that are more defining of your character. If you're a student, a project or assignment may be at the foreground, but the background is your education. It's almost like you're driving a car with the end goal of getting to a location north of you, but some of the roads require a turn east or west to get onto the right path.

The foreground is highly situational, and to cope, you develop certain mechanisms, as Goldstein calls them. We will use the more common term of *habits*. When making key decisions to move forward with the events happening in your foreground, your background provides your motivations and inhibitions, and will likely allow you to truly decide on the best actions moving forward.

Let's analyze a specific example, coming from the novel *The Life of Pi* by Yann Martel. The novel tells the story of Pi, who was stranded in the middle of the ocean with nothing more than a tiger on his boat, and it was crucial he assert his position in his environment. At the foreground were his basic needs, such as food and water, and at the background, his character, personality, and way of life he didn't want to change. Due to Pi's extenuating circumstances, he was forced to abandon his vegetarianism to stay alive; this was a necessary evil, and even though it would not have aligned with his self-actualization in his life prior to the shipwreck, it was now a necessary means of survival.

This brings us to our key point: circumstances can, and will, change. As they do, the brain responds accordingly, and scaffolding occurs that allows for a better future response, easing the discomfort and guilt that comes with change. Self-actualization is solely your personal reaction to your circumstances. Your environment is what will dictate what is important to you in each moment. If you are sick and dying, then the only aspect of life you can be focused on is living. You are not concerned with how much money you can make in the next ten years; rather, you are hoping to *live* for the next ten years. Living would indicate self-actualization *at that moment.*

This is also biologically founded. The brain can only focus on one *major* issue at a time. Multi-tasking has been found to be wholly ineffective (May and Elder, 2018). In the context of Goldstein's definition for self-actualization, it is actually the overabundance of disorder that the multiple focuses provide. Increased disorder brings about increased stressors, resulting in a hormonal reaction (associated with an adrenaline rush). This creates an environment where the organism has even less control, creating a vicious stress cycle and hindering the organism's immediate and more long-term potential success.

That is why we separate things by priority. Once you overcome the aforementioned sickness, your environment will change dramatically and there are new goals and aspirations, each of which will bring a new layer to your self-actualization.

These new layers to life are what interest and excite us. Think about the last time you got bored of doing something, whether it be filling out paperwork, cleaning, cooking, reading, listening to somebody talk, etc. Now think about the first time you performed that same action. The emotions are likely different because there was originally somewhere to progress. If you're a law student and you look at a law book for the very first time, you are probably fascinated by the simplicity of certain things and the complexity of others; if you're a secretary first learning your way around the office, things will be exciting. Two days, weeks, months, years, or even decades later, that action will eventually feel monotonous. This is because you've mastered, or at least nearly mastered, it.

Let's use the analogy on tug of war. I still remember the first time I played this game. It was in an enormous auditorium in my elementary school, around third grade. We all lined up on either side of the rope, a blaring sound went off over the loudspeaker, and we were suddenly pulling. This game is so simple and natural because it of its similarity to how we live life. When you pull, it is interesting. There is uncertainty in the future: Will you or your opponent win? If you're just standing there, holding the rope, it gets boring quickly. Thus, we must always maintain a certain level of tension in our lives, whether it be self-imposed or externally attributed, to allow us to continuously self-actualize. In life, the goal is not to get rid of the tension, but to level up and maintain the same firm grip. Progress will follow continuous self-actualization.

We will describe self-actualization as a process of maintaining pressure but releasing tension to the degree that will allow you to manifest your background in your foreground. If you sit around all day doing nothing, the rope will fall to the ground and may be too heavy to pick back up. There is a necessary balance or equilibrium uniquely present for *you*.

Return to the question I asked you in the introduction about defining success personally. If you achieved that goal, would you be your best self? Ideally, yes.

Your only and ultimate drive in life should be self-actualization. Everything else is a step to getting there.

Carl Rogers' Thoughts on the Process of Self-actualization
Psychologist Carl Rogers developed the theory that self-actualization is the fulfillment of the person's sense

of self, which could only be done through continuous reflection and reinterpretation of life. He touches on the values associated with the individual, as well as the relationships the individual builds, and notes the process of self-actualization is continuous. He points to the process of self-actualization as the ultimate form of fulfillment.

Rogers believed for a person to achieve self-actualization, they must be in a state of congruence. Congruence is achieved when a person's actual self and ideal self are similar (Ahmad and Tekke, 2015).

Maslow's Hierarchy of Psychological Needs

In 1943, Abraham Maslow first published his hierarchy of psychological needs, a pyramid-like system that focuses on what goes right in one's life and allows the individual to achieve the next "level." Unless an individual has fulfilled all the needs in a certain level, they cannot move on. Since then, Maslow's hierarchy of psychological needs has become a common source for explanation in the realm of positive psychology. The layers, with their now accepted contents, are pictured and described below:

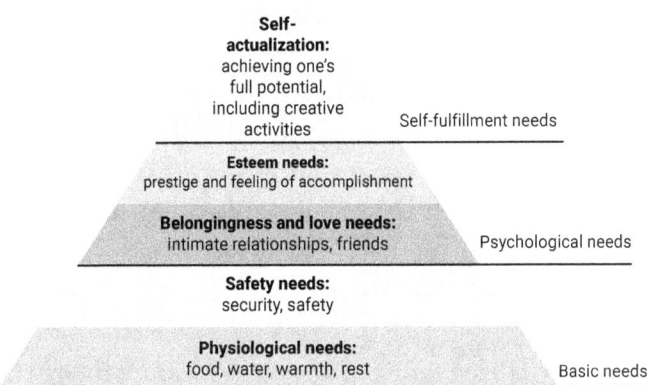

Maslow's hierarchy of needs

The basic human needs are at the very bottom, laying the foundation for everything to come. Once you have food and water, you can worry about security and safety. Relationships and accomplishments come after, with self-actualization only possible if all other aspects of life are fulfilled. This hierarchy has since been heavily criticized, as many people in the world do not have easy access to attainment of their basic needs, and yet they are happy.

Nonetheless, according to Maslow, self-actualization comes in the form of self-fulfillment, where the maximum potential of that person is achieved. Specifically, Maslow points out, "A musician must make music, an artist must paint, a poet must write, if he is to be ultimately at peace with himself. What a man can be, he must be." This is the essence of self-actualization in his eyes, with the underlying needs representing steppingstones that exist only to allow one to realize and become their true self. A key point to recognize about his theories is that he described self-actualization as a *desire* that leads to constantly changing ambitions, and constant fulfillment.

In Maslow's research, he believed there were nine self-actualized individuals from his time including Abraham Lincoln, Thomas Jefferson, and Albert Einstein, as well as Eleanor Roosevelt and Aldous Huxley (BigThink, 2019). He presented explanations for why each of them fits into this category, summarized below:

- Self-actualized individuals have a meaningful, harmless sense of humor.
- Self-actualized individuals believe in universal respect, accepting each human without judgment.
- Self-actualized individuals have a higher mission to fulfill that extends past the person themselves. They devote their lives to such missions.
- Self-actualized individuals have powerful moments that make them more self-aware. They perceive the world as it is, without influences from personal biases.
- Self-actualized individuals do not depend on material satisfactions or other people for satisfaction, but on continuous growth of their potentialities.

Maslow expressed less than 1 percent of the adult population will achieve self-actualization due to the insufficient fulfillment of basic needs, as well as the psychological insecurity and lack of relationship development many people are victims of. Throughout this book, you will learn all the habits you must incorporate into your life to allow you to fully self-actualize and beat the statistic.

In the game of tug of war, Maslow's hierarchical structure of needs is very applicable. You cannot play tug of war if your hands are sore from lifting heavy weights. This is an example of a phenomenon that would disturb you from your normal function and could distract you from your drive of maintaining your grip on the rope and constantly advancing. Pressing issues are now at your foreground that not only present themselves as immediate grabs for your attention, but also potential limitations for the fulfillment of your background desire to become your greatest self.

Although we will recognize Maslow's contribution to the term "self-actualization," we will not be using the core theory he provides, which is it is impossible to achieve self-actualization without fulfilling all of the previous tiers of the pyramid. Rather, in the context of all the future chapters, the first four tiers of Maslow's pyramid will act as a part of the self-actualization.

To better understand this, compare your life to a home. Your childhood experiences have molded your life in such a way there is a pre-set home you will receive around the age of twelve. Then, as you begin to make your own decisions and go through bigger and more future-shaping challenges, you can begin to change things in the home. With each change, the home gets better, and at certain points, it may even be exactly what you're looking for. Then, your preferences will change, and there is a new technology you may want to accessorize your home with. That means even though you already have a garage door, you just want to replace it with a new one. The same occurs in our lives when we self-actualize. The world keeps moving, and we are keeping up with it. Based on Maslow's hierarchy, we know what components of self-actualization are necessary, but it is not impossible to achieve the over-arching concept of self-actualization without *all* the tiers.

What Is the Drive to Self-actualization?

Paul Pagnato, a positive mental attitude (PMA) enthusiast, described a think group he was a part of, put together by Salim Ismael, the former architect behind Yahoo and the author of *Exponential Organizations*. This was a group of forty individuals from different backgrounds of academia, nonprofit, tech, etc., with equally balanced racial, religious, and gender distribution. The question Ismael proposed was, "What is the purpose of life?"

As Paul was telling this story, I thought back to a book I had read as a child, *Jeremy Fink and the Meaning of Life*, where the protagonist is searching for the secret to life and following a series of clues that are supposed to help her find the key to unlock the box containing the answer to this question her father had left for her. The author never actually reveals the contents of the box, and clearly this has left me pondering since, so it was a wonderful conclusion to the beautifully written book.

Paul and his fellow thinkers thought about this question more broadly, considering all forms of life: humans, viruses, bacteria, plants, insects—anything and everything that can be deemed "alive." They came up with a common denominator: Every organism's goal is to not go extinct. For this to happen, that species must grow, change, adapt, and evolve; otherwise, the threat of extinction is quite real.

With the context of this book, this constant growth and change create a positive feedback loop with the never-ending process of self-actualization. A positive feedback loop is a scientific term coined to describe a process where the products cause more of the reactant to be made, and thus the reactant pushes for more of the products to be made. The result: exponential growth, like cancerous cells. Think about the infinite positive possibilities that can come about from a cancer-like progression of the good things in life. This is how we will break down the term *drives*.

Drives, as Goldstein describes them, are tendencies that depend on potentialities. We are innately gifted with certain potentialities. These are things you will naturally be able to do better than anyone else around you; it's only a matter of identifying and working on them. When we identify potentialities, we will begin to notice the tendencies we have around them. Once this becomes a logical thought, there is now an innate desire to fulfill that potential—thus delineating the drive toward self-actualization.

Flow Chart to the Drive of Self-actualization:

Potentialities → Tendencies → Habits → Actions → Self-actualization

---

How Do I Get Started on My Path to Self-actualization?

A wonderful example of this progression is my friend and peer's approach to his projects. Nolan Siegel, a name that will likely be recognized by many by the end of his career, is a Vanderbilt student and a curious and dedicated thinker. Anyone who meets him knows he's always up to something, whether it be working on a project for research credit, exploring the applications of metaphysics in political science, or writing a 120-plus page paper on something originally given as a two-paragraph assignment.

This past semester, Nolan's directed study was with his astronomy professor, where he explored the difference between metaphysics and physics. Metaphysics was what Aristotle did when he looked up at the stars, saw they move in circles, and said, "The stars move in circles; therefore Earth must be special. We must be the center of the universe, and everything must revolve around us." He saw the evidence, and he came up with a why, which was unsubstantiated, but appeared to be substantiated based on his one observation. Essentially, he made the "why" match the "how."

Then we have physics, and Johannes Kepler said, "I can make the math work where the planets orbit the sun and ellipses, but I can't tell you why. But that's how the world works. That's how the universe, or the solar system works." Kepler had the how, but not the why. Today, we base our fundamental understandings of astronomy on Kepler's discoveries.

Nolan applied this knowledge of astronomy to his political science polling project, taking the potential of his research abilities, which he had discovered early in college, and adding on the habit of questioning the "why" and "how," as well as the basis of the correlations or conclusions he was making based on the data presented to him.

Nolan began working on his polling data project by looking at determinants of American political ideology, and how they shifted from year to year. The original goal was to investigate these shifts, with the background of national and global events in mind. As he wandered further into the research, he was expecting to find the financial crisis of 2008–2009 hit in the middle of a decrease in individual income, causing Americans to lean more left in their voting. There was an apparent impact on political ideology as the income went up because voters were then more likely to vote right.

At this point, Nolan is exploring his potentialities, combined with tendencies. He is naturally inclined toward approaching things in a methodical way, and by inspecting the various correlations between trends in data, he is creating tendencies. These tendencies to working on research projects become habits, as they have for Nolan. Self-actualization would be the result of the compounding of the habits in a way that optimizes his potential.

The research in itself is another example of achieving self-actualization. As humans, we are often inclined to take the route Aristotle did and make the evidence fit the conclusion, forcing the "why" onto the "what." There is *potential* for that theory to be correct, but it doesn't necessarily mean it is the correct path.

As Nolan continued to think through his work on this project, he was then able to separate himself from the unsubstantiated claims he was making to match the evidence. This allowed him to pivot to a better and more realistic observation with his project and create something scientifically based. This project was able to reach its full potential and self-actualize. It was the initial drive to be able to produce something Nolan could learn from that allowed him to finish it to the best of his ability.

Similarly, when a child is first learning to communicate, things are very difficult. It would be easy to give up, but once the child expresses a syllable, there is now an innate understanding that he/she is able to pronounce something. They have the encouragement of their family, their smiles and enthusiasm nudging them toward this goal; this A-team support makes it easier to keep pushing, and worth it. There is the potentiality of speaking in complete words, phrases, sentences, or paragraphs, like they've heard those around them speak for months. This child will begin to continuously enunciate more, with preference to certain syllables that are easier than others. This is the tendency stage.

Once the child can pronounce words, it becomes only habit of speaking all the time to build on their vocabulary, expand their lexicon, and fulfill their potential of communicating effectively. With each word, it becomes easier to do so, and allows the self-actualization of speaking easier; the child then has a stronger desire and drive to do so. Their A-team no longer praises them for pronouncing words, but for good grades, acts of kindness, or any other first. This praise acts as a motivator, maintaining the necessary tension in children's lives.

Of course, this will then turn into a life-long, continuous process of reading, writing, expressing oneself, learning more languages, etc. There is never an end, and there is always more to do. However, the drive toward self-actualization is displayed clearly through this step-by-step mentality.

Throughout life, if you continuously adopt certain habits, self-actualization is possible because the activities you partake in are a direct result of the habits you've implemented, all of which formed because of your potentialities.

Using the definition we have delineated, where self-actualization is a constant fulfillment of your personal potential, it is important to maintain a process of consistent re-evaluation. Whether at the foreground or background, Goldstein's, Maslow's, and Rogers' term allows us to rise into the beings we know we can be, but it is entirely up to us to act on these theories. In the upcoming chapters, we will go through the way to reach self-actualization, starting with the values Rogers mentions, which will be pivotal in defining your background. You will see how you can build on those values with the potentialities, habits, and actions you have already established, and ones you will establish in the future. Then you will be able to put them together to create a meaningful mission statement that is passionate and purpose driven, as well as adjustable based on any new environment you may find yourself in.

PART 1

GENEROSITY

Generosity (noun): an act of unselfish giving.

GENEROSITY

Do all the good you can,
By all the means you can,
In all the ways you can,
In all the places you can,
At all the times you can,
To all the people you can,
As long as ever you can.

—JOHN WESLEY

My sister is a hostess in one of the very well-known restaurants in our area, and it wasn't until she started working there that she was really able to understand the term *gratitude*. Imagine these two scenarios:

A woman, clutching her phone, yelling into the speaker about the bad service she just received and the money return she expects immediately, storms up to the front of the restaurant.

"How can I help you, ma'am?" my sister asks in an angelic voice she never uses at home.

"Great, I need a table for two. I'm in a rush, and last time I ate here, the food was absolutely awful. Don't do that again," the woman responds aggressively, and returns to her anger-fueled interaction.

At this point, my sister has a choice: She can either move some things around in the system and put in her best effort to seat this woman, who will likely leave a poor review and minimal tip, or she can say the restaurant is full.

Without a doubt, this is how this conversation will end: "I'm sorry, ma'am, the restaurant is full. The wait is currently a little over an hour," my sister says out loud, but thinks something completely different, and then smirks when the woman turns around and leaves.

Now imagine it went like this. The woman is still clutching her phone, still yelling, and still storming up to the front entrance. This time, she puts down her phone, mutes herself in the call, and smiles at the hostess.

"How can I help you, ma'am?" my sister asks in the angelic voice she never uses at home.

"Hi dear, could you please get me a table for two? My husband and I are going through an absolutely terrible time with renovations right now, and the constructor just laid down the tiles all wrong! Now I'll have to pay triple to remove it!" she expresses, sharing her concerns with the hostess, smiling in the process, even though she is clearly emotionally drained from the interaction.

"Oh no, I am so sorry to hear that! Let me see what I can do for you," my sister responds, and genuinely tries to move things around. "It looks like it may be around an hour wait, but I can try to seat you outside at one of the corner tables, if that works? We usually reserve those but would that be okay?" she proposes.

The woman expresses her thank yous, agrees to sit at that place, and the rest of the night goes exceptionally well. She comes up to my sister at the conclusion of her dinner and hands her an envelope with her *gratuity*.

There is a wonderful aspect of human empathy that falls under the umbrella term of generosity, defined vaguely as the willingness to give or share (Merriam Webster Dictionary). Between these two situations, there is a stark contrast between the generosity expressed by the woman from the beginning toward the hostess, the generosity the hostess expresses toward the woman in response, and then the gratitude the woman expresses at the end of the night through her tip. It is a revolving door creating a positive feedback loop that can be broken down into three parts.

Generosity

Gratitude toward others → actions that will make people appreciative of you → understanding that everyone is human

GRATITUDE

"It is not happiness that brings us gratitude. It is gratitude that brings us happiness."

Losing a job or missing a much-wanted opportunity is one example everyone can relate to. It feels like the end of the world, regardless of age, but the ending of something naturally necessitates the start of something new. Essentially, it is almost like the universe is making a path specifically designed for us because if you missed one thing, that just means something else is going to come. There is no way it isn't.

At the end of the day, we all have something to be thankful for. Whether it is family or friends, a job or a volunteering experience, a mental capability or a physical one, there is *always* a way to turn the situation around mentally and find something, anything, to be thankful for.

A recent interview with a man named Jeremy Strickland reminded me of all the little things one can be grateful for. As the chief of staff (go-to-market partner) to a senior leader who owns sales from eCommerce, Retail, and Search at Google, he works closely with the executive team. Strickland is a busy man. Still, between the festivities of New Years' preparations, he found the time to connect and schedule a meeting within twenty-four hours of me sending him a LinkedIn connection request. This was December 31, and it was a first for me.

Our interview went well, and it focused on the importance of gratitude.

"One of the things I've truly learned in my career is we don't express appreciation enough," he noted, and continued to do just that. "Thank you for your hard work, your time, your patience, and your interest."

I was so taken aback by this overwhelming amount of gratitude. "Why are you thanking me? I should be the one thanking you!"

"No. In every interaction, in every email, and just every possibility, you need to lead with gratitude," he concluded, and then followed up a few minutes later with an article relating to my book topic, as well as the repetition of the offer to connect me with others.

Looking back, the concluding three minutes or so were simply expressions of gratitude, but the emotions that came up as a result were powerful. Strickland thanked me for the opportunity being interviewed by me, wished me the best on my book-writing journey, and offered to connect me with other individuals who may be interesting case studies for the book. He thanked me for my time in preparing the questions and sending them over to him ahead of time, for forcing him to think, and for allowing him to think out loud at times.

This interaction is in no way exceptional by the measure of the effort required of Strickland. However, it *was* exceptional due to his decision to take that step. Two sentences made a significant difference in my day and created a positive feedback loop. I felt heard and appreciated, listened to, and validated for the time and effort I was putting into my passion project. I felt moved to show more gratitude toward not only Strickland, but also the next person I spoke to, who reciprocated this and continued the loop.

If gratitude were something we expressed day-to-day, we would be more patient, kind, and understanding. This is especially evident in the religious conditioning of gratitude and the effect it has on lifelong happiness.

Express gratitude day-to-day to truly feel the effects on your long-term happiness. Little things that may not mean anything to you could mean the world to those around you.

David Steindl-Rast is an American Catholic Benedictine monk, author, and lecturer who presented a TED Talk in 2013 on the relationship between happiness and gratefulness. He reverses the thought process so many of us have been instilled with: When you are happy, you are grateful. No, according to Steindl-Rast, "it is not happiness that makes us grateful; it is gratefulness that makes us happy."

This monk presents his compelling argument with the foundation that being given a valuable experience is something that inspires gratefulness. Every moment is an opportunity, a new gift. If you miss it, there will be another one, but you must be careful not to miss it.

That is why he falls back on a simple process to achieve gratefulness. It mirrors what we are taught in grade school about crossing the street. *Stop. Look. Go.* Stop to notice what is happening around you. Build stop signs into your life, and make it a hard stop. Then, look. Open yourself up and all your senses to smell the roses. "There is a wonderful richness that is given to us," he says. Ultimately, life is about enjoying what is given to us, and that is what brings us to the final step: go. Go and be happy. Be present in the flavors that life has to offer, and share them with others.

With the sometimes-overwhelming stressors of college life, I needed to build in numerous stop signs. A few of them have stuck. Every Friday night, I celebrate Shabbat with Vanderbilt Chabad, an organization I am proud to be a part of. This is a time to relax without technology, interact with other Jews, and really take in what this past week brought me.

The stop sign: Every Friday night, at 7:00 p.m., I have dinner with Chabad. No excuses.

The look: Put away the technology for a few hours, eat dinner, and chat. No exceptions.

The go: Chat with, hug, and enjoy the presence of those sitting around me. No worrying.

These weekly events are some of the moments I am most grateful for.

Gratitude becomes the solution. The solution to fear, and thus a cure for violence. It allows you to act out of a sense of "enough," which creates a culture of sharing. You begin to notice and enjoy the differences between people, emphasizing the importance of equality and equity in the modern world.

In Buddhism, there is a heavy emphasis on the importance of being grateful for the world around you, especially nature. Buddhist master Jack Kornfield has spent the last forty years studying and teaching Buddhism to the Western world. In terms of the degree to which gratitude exists in the spiritual practice, there is a prayer that asks for challenges (Gregoire, 2014).

> *"May I be given the appropriate difficulties so that my heart can truly open with compassion."*
>
> —Jack Kornfield

Imagine asking for that. Being grateful for not only life's blessing but also its suffering is a key component of living a spiritual life—and more broadly, to a fulfilling and meaningful life. To clarify, this does not mean you should wait for infliction to make a difference, but that if you do get inflicted, you should take it as an opportunity.

"There is no reason to be grateful for only the positive things because there is beauty in everything. There is beauty in pain, and in loss, as well as suffering," he says.

"We have the privilege of the lavender color at sunset, the taste of a tangerine in our mouth, and the almost unbearable beauty of life around us, along with its troubles. It keeps recreating itself. We can either be lost in a smaller state of consciousness—what in Buddhist psychology is called the 'body of fear,' which brings suffering to us and to others—or we can bring the quality of love and appreciation, which I would call gratitude, to life."

This ability to be grateful for something, despite the suffering associated with it, comes across in the story of Whitney Austin, who was entering the revolving doors of Fifth Third Bank headquarters only to fall into a slowed reality where twelve bullets were being fired at her, one by one. Since then, nothing about her life has been the same. Coming on to our call, she had been waiting for insurance to approve a CT myelogram to explore back pain because she cannot receive an MRI due to residual shrapnel in her body. Her life has been turned upside down, redefining her mission forever, but she remains optimistic.

"That experience brought me to where I am now professionally, and that stems from gratitude," she notes.

Reflecting on her childhood years, Whitney remembers doing a lot of volunteering, an act her dad regularly participated in and ingrained in the family dynamic from an early age. However, as Whitney progressed through life, got into college, and moved into the world of corporate America, she found herself devoting less and less time to the volunteering she cherished. There suddenly were other priorities: young babies, work, and simply a complete lack of time.

As Whitney was in free fall on September 6, 2018, all she could think about was how selfish she had been leading up to that moment. She was aware of the importance of her survival for the best outcome for her children, but there was also a spark that ignited a passion that had been dormant for so long.

"If I survive, I have to do something about this. I was not fine with gun violence before, but I wasn't so much concerned with taking action up to that point. I'd even taken some steps to sign up with an organization to help them, but the texts were coming to a more selfish Whitney, and she thought 'Oh, I don't have time for that.'"

This was monumental in Whitney's journey, and she made it her mission from that point to make a lasting impact. This solidified her identity as a positive person, and she turned the situation around mentally. Instead of thinking about her attacker as an individual to whom she must feel deep hatred, she is compassionate. She thinks about the situation as an opportunity to be connected to many people who are physically changed forever because of bullets, or those who have lost someone due to gun violence. She is purpose driven with the organization she founded, Whitney/Strong, which is steadfast in its mission of finding common ground to end gun violence through data-driven, responsible gun ownership solutions.

"I'm now full of gratitude, and I try my best to pay this gift forward."

Being grateful is a choice. Choose to immerse yourself in a grateful lifestyle and people around you will feel that.

There wasn't any clear explanation for Whitney's survival other than the heroism of the Cincinnati Police Department and trauma team at the University of Cincinnati Medical Center. There wasn't any rhyme or reason behind Whitney being the specific individual being shot. Whitney recognizes that and is able to think about this as an opportunity for a second life: one where she does everything to help others, where everything is different and there is the chance to make an impact, one where the feeling of gratitude for her survival motivates her each day to get up in the morning and take steps toward improving the safety of the community around her.

"If you could get to this mindset without getting shot, that is what I'd wish for anyone. This is something you'd want everyone to have: a responsibility to make things better. I don't know how you can get there easily without a life-changing experience," Whitney points out, while recognizing everything she has to be grateful for. She is alive. She made it home to her children and husband.

Just looking at Whitney's situation, it would seem difficult to find something to be thankful for, but she did. Now, she is much happier. She truly was able to put everything aside and find something to be thankful for.

Research notes the relationship between gratitude and happiness, as well. On a biological level, recent research in the field of emotions has found emotions carry a voltage. There is a vibrational frequency that resonates to a specific level that is associated with a certain emotion, and this results in a contraction or expansion of your life force. According to Dr. Shawna Freshwater, a PhD licensed clinical psychologist, neuropsychologist, and holistic practitioner, an increase in vibrational frequency results in an increase in expansion, and with it a greater Life Force in the individual's cells (Freshwater, 2017). When one feel enlightened, the highest frequency of 700-plus is achieved, and there is the greatest energy expansion; joy falls around 540, anger around 150, and that of depression is so minimal the cells create an energy vacuum, imitating lifelessness. Gratitude emits the same frequency as joy, coming in with a frequency around 540 MegaHertz, and can even stay around 900 MHz for short periods of time (Lesavich, 2019).

In psychology, "Gratitude is associated with a personal benefit that was not intentionally sought after, deserved, or earned but rather because of the good intentions of another person" (Emmons and McCullough, 2004). Never in her wildest dreams would Whitney have *asked* to be shot or go through the trauma associated with the change. Still, she was able to find something small to be grateful for in a truly unfortunate situation and allow this feeling of gratitude to grow.

This is a fundamental key to the exploration of gratitude in your life. Think about the last time you were ungrateful for something. Maybe you were stressed about a new role at work or a hard assignment in school. You certainly weren't happy about being given a hard deadline on short notice. How does thinking about this make you feel? Positively or negatively? Does it make you want to be grateful for your job, or question why you're still there?

Most likely, it is the latter, simply because of Hebb's Law. According to this scientific theory, the brain's neural connections can be molded by the mind and having certain thoughts over and over reinforces those connections. Due to the brain's plasticity, it is easy to create a new neural network after repeating a certain thought only a few times. Think about the first time you did basic math. Once two plus two was a novel concept, and your fingers were your guide to figuring this out. Once four became the clear answer, and one that you could elicit naturally, that reflected a neural connection being made.

The same applies to gratitude. If you are consistently expressing gratitude, your brain will be perceptive and start meshing the brain matter together in a specific way that will make it easier for you to express gratitude in the future. Each time you are placed in a situation, your brain will naturally go down the strongest neural connection. With each time you express gratitude, you strengthen the connection that allows for a response reflecting appreciation, making this a more immediate choice in the future. This creates a positive feedback loop.

As Emily Fletcher, founder of Ziva and creator of the first online meditation training program states in her publication, "Over time, this encourages our brains to more consistently search for the constructive themes in our life instead of the destructive ones, helping us water the flowers instead of watering the weeds" (Fletcher, 2015).

Indeed, many studies over the past decade have found people who consciously count their blessings tend to be happier and less depressed. Gratitude as a regular act is emphasized in all the primary monotheistic religions (Peterson and Seligman, 2004).

For example, in Judaism, the expression of gratitude is instilled in daily activities, grounding the faithful to a recognition that they are reliant on those around them, and the world only functions with the help of gratitude. The *Modeh Ani* is a prayer said upon waking up, before doing anything else, and it thanks G-d for the gift of life ("Modeh Ani: What and Why"). The blessings on food, and those following a meal, the *Birkat Ha Mazon*, thank those who prepared the meal, those with whom we ate, and G-d (Borovitz, 2019). A major notion in the religion is *hakaras hatov*, meaning appreciation and recognition of the good that G-d does for you, extending to appreciation of all the people around us. With each prayer, the thought of gratitude becomes more ingrained, and the effects of the act are additive (Touger).

This idea of gratitude is not foreign to us. Americans yearly sit down around the dinner table, turkey front and center, and politics ready to be discussed. The holiday of Thanksgiving brings overwhelming feelings of thankfulness to the room, where families discuss the aspects of their lives they are thankful for. But according to psychologist David DeSteno, who has conducted tens of research studies on the topic of gratitude, as well as published numerous books and given various talks on the topic, believes that the positive effects of gratitude are simply wasted on this holiday (DeSteno, 2019).

Think about it this way: If you decide you are going to be grateful for everything in your life once a year, it is comparable to eating healthy one day out of the year. There is not going to be a significant change in your day-to-day life because you are not forming any habits. If anything, it may seem like a pain to go through the process only to continue life as normal the following day. This is something DeSteno's research supports: Gratitude can produce significant differences in our levels of honesty, self-control, and productivity. *But that is only if it is a constant occurrence.* At its core, gratitude allows us to build connections, and those don't happen in one day.

All these rules also apply to complaining and subsequently, constant negative feelings. If you keep complaining and finding negativity in situations, your brain is going to be wired that way and it will become a way of life. Take a moment to think about something you complained about recently. It can be something trivial, or something that really weighs down on you. For me, something that has been very anxiety inducing for the last few weeks was the prospect of going back to school and starting the routine of engineering classes again. It is really difficult for me to do well in these courses and stay positive throughout the semester, especially with COVID-19 and virtual offerings.

Now, take whatever situation you just thought of and turn it around. What are you grateful for in that instance? How can this affect you positively? How is this an opportunity for growth, change, and prosperity? In my situation, I am incredibly fortunate to have access to an elite education, and be surrounded by like-minded individuals who are kind, understanding, and collaborative.

Finally, reflect on what felt better: the complaint (the negative thought) or the act of gratitude (the positive thought). Personally, I am a complainer, so I know how difficult this can be, but it is certainly the latter that provides me with that warm feeling I strive to maintain inside.

This process is one you should go through daily, if for no reason other than to create a positively thinking neural network that will allow you to experience gratitude more frequently and deeply. Remember that things will be hard, but the positive effects of gratitude are immense, something that has been proven time and again throughout history, religion, and scientific research. Let yourself be grateful and put yourself in the position to do so optimally. *Always* find something to be grateful for.

APPRECIATION THROUGH ACTION

God gave you a gift of 86,400 seconds today. Have you used one to say thank you?

—WILLIAM ARTHUR WARD

When I was younger, my mom would say there are little fairies all around us making sure the balance of good and evil is maintained. For every good thing you did, the fairies would recognize that and reward you. For every bad action you took, they would punish you. Right after I'd say something nasty to my sister, I'd trip over something. It's always the fairies! As I grew older, I learned other people refer to this as karma.

Karma is a law in Indian religion and philosophy under which any actions will impact your future existence (Brittanica). The term comes from the Sanskrit word *karman*, which is literally translated to "act." A good act is rewarded and a bad one is punished. The concept of karma is interesting because it implies whatever you put into the world is what you receive as a result. Dr. Jennifer Rhodes, a licensed psychologist, suggests that karma is the net total of the situations and interactions, each of which brings us either closer or takes us further away from our higher purpose, or self-actualized self (Lindberg, 2020).

The key to unlocking good karma: taking actions with positive consequences, chief among which is the act of appreciation.

Appreciation is the expression of gratitude through specific actions, and it can come up in the form of an action or through an investment. An action may be something small, like saying "thank you," or buying flowers or chocolates. It builds on gratitude, as gratitude is a feeling; Appreciation is a way to act on that feeling. The relationship between gratitude and appreciation is a positive feedback loop: the more grateful you feel, the more appreciative you are likely to act. In other words, your positive emotions will inspire action. Then it is up to you to take those actions—*that* is the key to a generous, and thus fulfilling, lifestyle.

While many of us feel gratitude, if we do not act on it, the other person will not perceive it. This means that they will not necessarily respond the way you want them to. Thus, it is necessary to *act*.

Sometimes, this action can even be granting someone your time. In the process of conducting interviews for writing this book, the one thing that surprised me the most was how willing people were to speak to me. Individuals with crazy lives, appointments leading into the next year, with maybe a few minutes to spare, were sitting down to chat, at times for over an hour. This was a way of tipping their hat in my direction, making me feel grateful for their time, advice, and attention, and proactively building their network in a way that was mutually beneficial.

In my life, there is one person who is always showing appreciation for others. Olga Orak is a real estate agent who always has a smile on her face and is constantly willing to help others. When my parents were getting divorced and my mother was looking for a new home, Orak took on a new role: a mix of agent, friend, comforter, and general supporter. This extended to my siblings and me, as well. I still remember the numerous times Orak would come by our house, each time bringing a box of munchkins from Dunkin', which she would always get right before coming. Even if she was dropping off paperwork for my mom, something that took less than a minute and could easily be a passing exchange, her generosity was endless, and it was met with appreciation.

She tells a story of one scenario where her personal appreciation for her clients resulted in a comical and legal break-in. Orak had been relaxing by her pool, and she gets a call from her client.

"Listen, I'm already in the city, but I think I left the stove on in my house. You can't go in through the garage because it doesn't automatically open, and I have the keys to the front door." Bewildered, Orak asked what she was meant to do in this situation. "Oh, my kitchen window is open!"

Orak packed up her things, drove over to her clients' home (which was about thirty minutes away), and started to engineer a way to climb through the kitchen window. "I got a chair from the backyard and crawled right through! I had to go out the same way because there was no other way for me to lock all the exits from the outside," Orak laughed.

Unsurprisingly, Orak's actions did not go unnoticed in the Central Jersey community, where Orak quickly became the most sought-out realtor, receiving awards for her sales and her kindness. For her, it is about a constant show of appreciation for her customers: each one is treated in the best way, like a friend. For my mom, it was bringing her children munchkins and brightening up their day. For others, it is climbing through their kitchen window to make sure the stove is off. On Facebook, it means wishing each and every person she comes in contact with the very best, especially on their birthdays and on special holidays. The cycle for Orak is natural because of the consistency of action.

Consistency of action will make those around you feel appreciated, and they will express gratitude toward you. This will make your path to happiness a shorter one.

This necessity of action is something Becca Stevens, founder of Thistle Farms, understands all too well. She started her career as an Episcopal priest, but something she has always valued was freedom—freedom for herself and those around her. She would visit women in jail and help women on the streets. A realization was dawning upon her that the systems we had in place were not serving the survivors of trauma, but rather re-traumatizing them. There was a lack of informed care, and verbiage toward survivors was cruel and derogatory. This was the mental process Stevens was going through, and she had good intentions, but she was not acting on them in a way that was very effective.

A trip to downtown Nashville with her four-year-old son changed these thoughts into actions. There was a big sign for the local strip club that said, "Classic Cat," and a barely covered woman was pictured smiling. Her son asked her, "Mama, why is that lady smiling?" and Stevens felt spurred to act.

"I looked up and it broke my heart because I was thinking, someday, he's not going to ask that question… I knew in that moment I wanted him to see something different. I wanted him to think there is a different way of honoring and loving women, supporting them in the best way possible." She noted a lot of women are forced into "adult entertainment" against their will and that's where the problem lies.

Thus, Thistle Farms, a ministry that helps women in vulnerable places, specifically those who have been prostituted, imprisoned, assaulted, or abused, emerged. They reside in homes called Magdalene Houses and create products that are now sold at Whole Foods stores nationally. Thistle Farms has 532 beds around the country and ninety-two sister organizations established so far (Thistle Farms).

For Stevens, it comes down to showing love in the right way. As the author of ten books and counting, she emphasizes the healing qualities of love. Love is action. Love is helping people (Dinner Conversations). It is giving them the opportunity to go through their healing journeys. With her messaging and action, Stevens has impacted hundreds, if not thousands, and created dynamic change in the communities she is present in. Again, it all comes down to being proactive in respect to the needs of others.

Love is action. Show your love toward others by acting on it.

This is the traditional view on showing appreciation and comes naturally for *givers*. However, not all of us are givers (Grant, 2016).

Givers compose about 20 percent of the population, and to them, it is easier to focus on the needs of others than their own. Another 20 percent of the population are takers, which is the opposite of a giver, and they in turn will prefer to receive more from others than they will give in return (Cramm, 2014). The rest of the population is composed of matchers, who recognize and equalize the natural push and pull of relationships, and thus will maintain the balance of givers and takers.

In Judaism, this can be explained with the concept of the Tzaddik, Rasha, and Biononi. Each person has two souls: the animal, which draws out a person's desires and is a source of temptation, and the human, which connects to spiritual pleasures. The Tzaddik is simply a divine soul, almost like a spiritual superhero. In the context of the giver and taker, this would be the giver. The Rasha is a person operating on impulse, where the animal soul has a strong hold, and the person will bow to physical pleasures. This would resemble the taker. The Biononi has temptations and challenges, but has mastered self-control, not allowing the animal soul to control their life. The Biononi is the objective, and it is something each person is encouraged to work toward, to eventually have a seamless connection with oneself by recognizing the importance of helping the world around them (Jewish Learning Institute, 2020).

Judaism suggests the Biononi must strive to be better because they can be better. The taker will often find it a difficult venture to show appreciation. This does not make a taker as an individual any better or worse than a giver. It is just how this individual is hard-wired, and there are certain effects of having this personality type. Specifically, this can make them less respected in the workplace, and less well-liked in personal relationships that require fifty-fifty input for success. Thus, a taker needs to reframe their thinking to be able to "give" to those around them while maintaining their identity as someone who "receives." It is much easier than it sounds: Think about what you can get out of giving someone something (i.e., your time, energy, patience, money, advice, etc.) in the long run. It's almost like a long-term investment.

> *Anyone can be a better version of themselves, and that starts by thinking outside of yourself.*

This is a tactic often used in politics, management, and even education.

In one of my interviews, I spoke with Ike Lawrence Epstein, current senior executive vice president and chief operating officer at the Ultimate Fighting Championship (UFC), who is responsible for all global business operations in the company, and he emphasized the long-term investment opportunities crucial to relationship building. As a public figure representing a billion-dollar enterprise, Epstein has become an expert at recognizing when it is necessary to invest in people, organizations, and next steps. He emphasizes the need to *be proactive*.

When COVID-19 started taking over the globe, many businesses were seeing a very bleak future. For athletic organizations, this was especially so: The athletes could not come together to practice or play, spectators could not fly in to watch and cheer them on, and the media were not allowed in public spaces. Athletic commissions around the country were no longer operating. Although a setback for Epstein, and the UFC, this was also an opportunity to create meaningful change and contribute to the community.

"One of the things I try to do with our elected officials is try to answer questions before they're asked," Epstein points out. COVID-19 provided the company with the chance to feature their ability to strategize, and they began working remotely as soon as offices closed. The very first action was to develop a game plan for returning to work. This resulted in a thirty-page document that was a "COVID-19 Operations Manual" of sorts, which Epstein and his team were able to present to the government. They went into depth about capacity requirements for stadiums, testing procedures, practice schedules, shut down possibilities, and more. Rather than demanding their company be reopened or requesting the timeline for operations and how the process of re-opening would occur, the UFC did the opposite. They were proactive with their planning, and they chose to make an investment. Plan now, help those who you ultimately rely on, and show your appreciation for the collaboration that will come as a result.

> *Showing appreciation means being proactive by investing in others. Don't wait for people to come to you; come to them. You need to be proactive.*

Indeed, there was ample appreciation that came following the presentation of the proposal. When they first presented the proposal, it was simply noted as something to look at *when the electeds were ready*. There was no time requirement, no nudge in any direction, no one asked them to do it. It was simply a show of good faith. Remember—gratitude will emerge only from actions taken without being explicitly asked, paid, or forced to do so.

What Epstein did in this case is exactly what being proactive in your appreciation means: Take a step to help someone, without them asking you for it. Don't ask for anything in return. More likely than not, they *will* remember to return the favor.

When the time came to think about starting to re-open, the UFC was ready. They had a safe and thought-out plan that could be used by the government for other organizations, if need be. Because they had invested early on, they were now two steps ahead in providing their entertainment to the public safely, and the government was now appreciative of the work the organization had put in.

Here, you are hopefully beginning to understand the backward approach to appreciation: If you cannot find a way to force yourself to show kindness or gratitude toward someone or something else, think about how it can benefit you in the long run. This is not an attitude that people like to take, but it is how the world works. The sooner you accept it, the better you will be at it. Think about the following questions before questioning whether being appreciative is worth it. Who might this person know? How may your relationship be able to help you get access to friends, resources, new information or perspectives?

It might seem selfish thinking about helping someone else to gain something as a result. According to the descriptive theory of psychological egoism, though, humans are inherently motivated by self-interest, and those who help others do so because of possible direct or indirect personal benefits (Stanford Encyclopedia of Philosophy). Many examples of how this not true might be running through your mind. There are surely people in your life who act graciously on instinct, without hesitation ("Tzaddik, Rasha & Beionini"). In both psychology and religion, there is a simple explanation for this called practice. With the right environment where societally beneficial actions are praised, an individual will seek to gain positive reinforcement for the good they do. This eventually becomes habit.

> *Humans will act selfishly, motivated by their self-interest. Make appreciation toward others part of your self-interest and you will find it easier to show gratitude day-to-day.*

At the end of the day, it is important to be proactive and invest in relationships. Find a way to give to others, even if it does not come naturally to you, because it will benefit you in the long run. You could be directed to a restaurant where you meet your soul mate or given a book recommendation that changes your life path. At a gathering last year, I was talking about a book I just finished reading and someone overheard. They had just finished reading the same one! We are now very close friends and talk daily. Who knows? Life works in mysterious ways but being proactive with your acts of appreciation will lead to others being helped as well. Do so by *acting*.

The key to developing appreciation as a habit is to make time in your calendar. There is *always* time to hold the door for the person behind you, to say "please" and "thank you," and other small actions. Here are some examples:

1. Once you meet someone, you need to remember their name. If you do not, ask for them to spell it. Repeating it out loud will not only help you remember, but it will also reinforce their mental and emotional connection to you. This is a sound they have heard since birth, and it has been scientifically proven that repetition causes familiarity, and familiarity is associated with positive emotions (Zhan Lexia et al., 2018). Just like seeing an ad multiple times will make you feel like you've already used the product, repeating someone's name will make them feel more comfortable with you.
2. If for any reason at all the date of someone's birthday comes up, add it to your calendar and *follow up*. This is the one day in the year that is entirely about that individual, and you notifying them that you are aware and ready to celebrate their existence is a demonstration of your appreciation that they are a part of your life (even if it is in the most menial way). I keep a separate calendar on my Google Calendar devoted to just birthdays. Whenever they come up, a quick "Happy birthday! Wishing you all the best this upcoming year!" will do the trick.
3. Everyone loves food. If you are working late with a team, or you are managing a group that needs to work overtime, you need to show them how much you appreciate their efforts. Yes, they may be getting paid for their hard work. Yes, there may be bonuses associated with the extra work they are putting in. However, there is nothing that says immediate

gratification better than a late-night dinner order, a quick bagel breakfast, or a surprise team outing to celebrate everyone's hard work. Remember the things in the workspace that make you grateful and use that to inform your actions.
4. Keep in touch with everyone. No one likes to feel used, and the best way to do that is to only turn for them when you have some sort of problem. The key to avoiding this is maintaining relationships (Riess, 2017). Holiday cards and messages are a quick way to check in. If you need to, have a spreadsheet of the people you meet and a key detail about them, if you are forgetful. It can be a wife or husband's name, the dog they have, or their children's new extracurricular activity. Remember one key detail and follow up at least once a year.

With time, these will become more natural and less of a hassle. These are points to jump off from, but you can do other things as well.

My grandfather is a man who is constantly showing his appreciation to everyone around him, and if he could give away his own skin, he most certainly would. When I was younger, I would go to summer camp very early in the morning and return around three in the afternoon. Each afternoon, he would walk up the giant hill that connected the path from our apartment to the bus stop and wait for me at the stop with some freshly bought ice cream. This was a secret between the two of us, and it was an expression of his care for me, as his granddaughter. Out of the memories we have together, it is definitely the little things I remember, like the vanilla ice cream with fruit syrup.

Similarly, the people around you will remember the little things.

As Stephen Covey, author of *7 Habits of Highly Effective People*, explains, "Next to physical survival, the greatest need of a human being is psychological survival—to be understood, to be affirmed, to be validated, to be appreciated. When you listen with empathy, you give that person the 'psychological air' to be all of these things."

The gratitude you feel toward others will be something you will be creating in others toward you by acting. If you are consistently proactive, it will become a habit, rather than a nuisance, and you will feel the effects of their gratitude for your presence in others' lives. Your generosity now is the translation of your gratitude for others into appreciation, and these little actions of appreciation will be received as a show of care. In due time, the recipients of your appreciation will reciprocate, keeping the positive feedback loop of gratitude and appreciation going.

UNDERSTANDING

Just because you don't understand something doesn't mean it's nonsense.

—LEMONY SNICKET

When was the last time you thought about the reason why the weather presents itself in the way that it does? The intricacies of all the preceding events that had led up to the rain or snow: temperature fluctuations, water evaporation and condensation, regional climate shifts, air pressure, and even the Earth's tilt toward or away from the sun. All these details needed to come together in perfect harmony to produce a rainstorm, blizzard, hurricane, or even a rainbow.

Now consider your reaction to each of these things on their own. For myself, I know that rain falling from the sky is no longer something special, but rather a complete pain to deal with. It means taking out my rain boots, preparing for my hair to go all over the place, and knowing that my already impeccable driving skills will be put to a further test.

The same goes with snow, but take yourself back to the first time you experienced snow. Not in the movies, or in any way other than physically standing outside and feeling the cool snowflakes land on your face, instantly melting. Consider the smile, representing pure and utter joy, that moment brought you.

When was the last time you thought about the reason the weather presents itself in the way that it does? Why do people present themselves in the way that they do?

Apply this same logic to the real world, where each person presents themselves in their own unique way. You do not know where they have been, or what they have experienced. You do not know the stories behind their smile or frown, or the thousands of years through the ancestral lineage that carry joy, pain, love, and suffering. You are not aware of the reasoning behind someone cutting you off, or why someone else pushed past you in a rush in the morning. Often, these things feel personal, but there could be a million reasons that led up to their action. Maybe they had a long day and just want solitude, or a loved one got into trouble. The point is, you will never exactly comprehend that person, in that form, in that setting, ever again. Treat every occurrence as unique, and this will serve as the grounding point in your understanding of others, pushing your generosity to its limits.

By doing so, you remove yourself from your own bubble, opening your life up beyond the biases you may currently have. This creates a positive feedback loop: You are understanding with someone, you learn more about their situation, you lose certain biases, which makes it easier to be understanding. This fits in with Frederickson's broaden and build theory that positive emotions broaden people's thinking, allowing them to be more receptive to new ideas, and build the individual into a new person (Frederickson, 1998). Since positive emotions are not pigeon-holed to specific threatening situations, the mind has the capacity to learn and then more effectively face life's challenges, in turn making the individual healthier and more fulfilled (Frederickson Barbara et al., 2008).

The concept of true understanding comes across in one of Jonathan Darling's recent experiences. Darling is a motivational speaker who preaches love as the new form of leadership, and he certainly acts on what he speaks about. One day he was at the checkout line in Sam's Club, which is always a crazy time because everyone is trying to push through. There was a couple checking out in front of Darling, and the checkout girl was clearly new. She was trying her best, but she certainly did not know what she was doing because she kept messing things up. With each new mistake, she was becoming more flustered, and the man who was checking out at that moment was not giving her the time of day. He urged her to hurry up, pointing out how easy her job is and her inability to do something extremely basic. After a few minutes, Darling could no longer contain himself.

"Sir, I think she gets it. You're frustrated; you're upset. But, you know, she's new," Darling pointed out to the man standing in front of him giving the girl a difficult time. In response, the man began to attack Darling, pointing out this was the checkout girl's job and she is not doing anything correctly.

"Sir, I get it," Darling responded, "but even you were new at something one day. I really hope when you were screwing up on the things you were new at, you had somebody who was willing to be incredibly patient." This caused the man to pause, clearly stumped, and turn around to face ahead, silent now.

The girl mouthed the words "thank you," and breathed a huge sigh of relief. Darling had led with love and had treated the girl with a level of understanding she was not treating herself with, and the impatient man certainly was not. In this moment, Darling solidified himself as a mini mentor, to both the checkout girl to be patient with others moving forward, and to the man in front to be kinder and more understanding.

Opportunities for mentorship will present themselves in a variety of ways. One of these is through mini mentors. It can be a single interaction with a person, an observation, a video, or an email. Any experience that you learn from fits in this category.

Orak tells a similar story about a first experience of hers. She was closing her first deal, at the point at which the realtor has to release the check given by the buyer from the escrow account. Orak was sitting there with the attorney and the other members of the team, waiting to receive her commission check. The attorney then asked, "Where is the escrow check you got from your clients?"

Orak was not aware that two copies of the check were supposed to be released. This confusion was written all over her face, and the attorney recognized that.

"Oh, I totally forgot! You already gave it to me!" the attorney smiled, calming Orak down. In that moment, he solidified himself as a mini mentor in her life.

"He knew I had forgotten it, but he didn't want to make me feel bad in front of team. It's stories like that which make you realize the importance of supportive people in your life who understand," Orak commented on the situation.

This form of mini mentorship is still ingrained in Orak's mind, and the understanding he showed her at the beginning of her career has given her valuable perspective and kept her grounded even since so many years have passed. Although this was a fleeting second that made such a huge impact in Orak's life, it shows it doesn't take much effort or time for this sort of mini mentorship. It's more of a way of life.

This idea of understanding is something we often diminish because we are so focused on where we are today. Today, you may be a successful businesswoman in a Fortune 500 company, but ten years ago, you were a student just like anyone else. Or you are now a student at a top-tier university, but two years ago, you were desperately putting together final drafts of your Common Application, in hopes of being granted admission to your dream school. We all have pasts, and we are all sometimes in situations where one kind word of understanding can change the entire progression of the day.

There is an element of humility to it. You are now at the point that you are, but you are still conscious of your limitations; this makes it easier for you to be patient and understanding with those around you. Research shows effective leaders routinely express humility, and in doing so they add value to firms, foster more welcoming team climates, and prioritize growth and development. This increases employee satisfaction, work engagement, and performance (Owens, Johnson, and Mitchell, 2013).

There are a few aspects to the humility that comes with understanding, namely a willingness to be self-aware, a visible appreciation for others, and the desire and willingness to be taught (Yang, Zhang, and Chen, 2019). Expressing humility improves interpersonal interactions and has a positive influence on those around them. Similarly, showing understanding will draw people in because it will make you relatable, approachable, and a pleasure to be around.

Think about it rationally. Would you rather people like you and want to be around you because they believe you are a good person, or avoid you at all costs because they fear you or dislike your character? According to rational choice theory, after weighing the benefits and drawbacks of each of these, most people will choose the former (Hechter and Kanazawa, 1997).

> *Everyone puts their pants on one leg at a time. Keep this in mind to keep you humble, and understand everyone has their own process, logic, and reasoning, but we all have one thing in common: We're human.*

This is something one of my professors, Dr. Piran Kidambi, emphasized in the first lecture of the course. He spent the first lecture and a half making us feel comfortable with him and the room, something rarely done by college professors in general, much less an engineering professor. However, he did something I thought was unique: we made name tags! Never would I have expected a junior-level core engineering college course instructor to tell us to create name tags on the first day of class. He did this, but with a twist. Both sides of the vertically folded paper would have our name written on them; one side would have a little star in the corner. If you set up the name tag in such a way that the side with the star faces the professor, then he will not call on you.

"We all have bad days, and my job is not to make it even worse by calling on you. Give me this non-verbal signal, and I'll leave you alone for the day," he explained.

We were shocked. A professor who not only heavily emphasized in-class participation, but also made us create name tags that would respect our personal boundaries. It was almost like we were on the same level: humans.

Professor Kidambi took this one step further. His actions in the first day of class provided a foundation of trust, which allowed him to start building his expectations.

With each class, the material increased in difficulty, but he *truly* made sure no student was left behind. The first few minutes of the class were spent on going over the material and how it all connected, there was a time when he asked for honest and critical feedback, and he solved the homework with us, step by step. There was an understanding: He put in the time, and we put in the effort. He even offered to reschedule the exam that fell on my birthday.

This is the sort of small indication of understanding for others' emotions that will make a dramatic difference in the lives you have the power to impact. If you are a manager, it is possible to lead with love, as Jonathan Darling suggests. If you are a professor, it may be recognizing and respecting the emotions of the students.

This respect and recognition that comes with understanding has been shown to improve performance in the classroom. More teacher support has been tied to students feeling more enjoyment, interest, and pride in their work, as well as reduced anxiety, depression, shame, anger, worry, boredom, or hopelessness (Lei, Cui, and Chiu, 2017). Feeling positive emotions like this is in turn linked to greater academic interest and effort and achievement (Valiente, Swanson, and Eisenberd, 2012).

Flexibility and improved conditions that are more reflective of the employees' needs have led to a shift in company culture. Companies such as Facebook, Microsoft, Apple, and Google have made a name for themselves globally due to their campaigns for mental health, pushes for collaboration in the workplace, and conditions that cater to the needs of employees as people (Shend, 2018). At Google, employees have access to free meals, laundry, and gym facilities, paid parental leave, and on-site childcare. There is also the additional flexibility of working on passion projects, and the company's support of the employee to be a teacher or coach to a fellow worker (Gillett, 2016).

Surprisingly, though, understanding is not necessarily built into our daily lives. We are busy, focused on our own worries, our own needs, our own schedules; our worlds revolve around ourselves. Judaism proposes an alternative: We are all here today, which means we are all the same today. When you engage in a kind act that is holy, such as understanding, you elevate everything around you to a higher level. In the Indian religions, an act of understanding gets you good karma.

This elevation, or good karma, is often something we are too busy to emphasize as necessary. That is why it sometimes takes a life-disrupting event to create this mutual understanding that should already exist day-to-day.

After Hurricane Sandy hit the coasts of New Jersey, communities came together in a level of understanding that had not been seen for many years. My entire neighborhood lost power, so one of my neighbors, who has a generator, welcomed everyone with open arms.

There was an unspoken agreement to be more kind and patient than ever. I remember my mother cooking rice and massive trays of chicken on the gas-powered stove and then bringing it over to our neighbors for dinner. Others went out and stood in line for hours in hopes of getting some gasoline, which they bought in large quantities to bring back home and share with others in the neighborhood. Some could not contribute anything to our large gathering, and that was acceptable.

There was an *understanding*: Everyone was figuring out the best was to maneuver the strange situation of living without electric power for nearly a month in the middle of a Northeastern winter. Schools were out, and the teachers in the neighborhood put together study groups and tutoring sessions to engage the children. This neighbor was cooking, cleaning, and housing everyone with a smile.

Ultimately, the ability to show understanding for others becomes a battle of "ego" versus "eco." On one hand, there is you. You are the individual, and largely concerned with your survival. On the other hand, there is the entire ecosystem that is impacted by your behavior. You rely on your ecosystem for resources, and the quicker you can recognize that, the better off you will be.

This same neighbor has always been a big proponent of the "eco," and has stepped up numerous times to help everyone in our community. Specifically, there was one summer my entire family was ready to go for our summer vacation. We were completely packed, loaded the car with our suitcases, and were off! The upcoming two months were going to be family time, spent with our grandparents on the beach. Little did we know that arriving at the airport would present us with the following challenge: My mom had left her suitcase at home. In the frantic hurry of packing everyone else up, she had forgotten her own items, and now would be left without clothes for the duration of our stay.

Quickly, my mom contacted our neighbor, who made her way to our house, entered through our garage, found the suitcase, and then drove about an hour and a half each way to bring us the forgotten suitcase. Never had someone been so committed to helping us out. We were not family, nor were we particularly close. Still, this was a woman who understood the level of stress my mother was under: traveling alone with three children under the age of ten, packing everyone up, and then noticing something was wrong only an hour before the start of boarding. She sympathized and was able to resolve the situation. Since then, and for numerous other reasons, we have been quite thankful for her.

What would we look like if we were constantly this understanding? What long-term impact would we be able to have on the people around us? How quickly could we change the world in a positive and meaningful way?

Understanding is being patient, regardless of the circumstances. Change thoughts from "How is this affecting me?" to "What is this person going through?"

There is a lot to learn from each of these examples but they are, ultimately, just off hand interactions, unique responses by a highly understanding individual in situations of stress. While we can look at them and take away their lessons, the value of surrounding ourselves with such people, or becoming them through constant acts of kindness, is far greater. We will call them our "A-team."

The A-team is the people you surround yourself with who 1) keep you grounded and make you feel loved with their support, and 2) do not let you fall into a state of inertia. These are individuals who appreciate your potential and have the capacity to shape your future. This is because of the Law of Averages, a theory that states the outcome of any situation will be the average of all the possible results. Similarly, as motivational speaker Jim Rohn said, humans are the average of the five people they spend the most time with. If you choose to surround yourself with people who are unmotivated, lazy, unkind, rude, and lacking in empathy, then you are more likely to mirror their behavior. If you find yourself in a circle of overachievers, gracious individuals, and trustworthy mentors, you are one step closer to your self-actualized form.

The beautiful thing about the A-team is that they recognize you are human and you can, *and will*, make mistakes. They will be generous with their understanding. They will be patient and allow you to blossom into your truest form. This is a community that grants you the space to show appreciation toward others and fosters a positive feedback loop of gratitude and appreciation.

For Jodi Anderson, having an A-team helped him separate himself from crime entirely and devote himself to getting an education. While in prison, Jodi had the opportunity to be a part of Cornell's Prison Education program, which educated incarcerated individuals and provided them with the opportunity to receive an undergraduate education. Once Jodi made the decision to take on this alternative path, everyone around him recognized and supported that. There was a mutual agreement those who he had been helping for so many years would step up and support him.

"They would feed me, provide clothing, and take care of everything. I didn't have to go into combat, and I don't have any scars because of that."

This eliminated the worries of transportation and recognized this was ultimately an intentional decision the young man was making to turn his life around. This was the power of the A-team, the group he had become a part of from home and grew to rely on over the years.

Others, however, also became essential components of Jodi's life, and have allowed him to flourish since despite his past. This became particularly apparent in Jodi's struggle to take required college admissions testing. He signed up for the SAT and arrived on time and ready to take the test. There was only one small problem: He had not printed the ticket, and this was required for admission. Thus, the SAT score was a failure, and he had to start looking at other options.

Then, Jodi discovered the ACT, an alternative to the SAT. There was hope! Hope was two states away, though, and

Jodi was not allowed to leave the county, much less be out after dark. Jodi's hope dissipated and left him feeling dejected and even more upset than before. Without the help of his A-team, Jodi would have gone to community college and likely returned to the life of crime that seemed so familiar at that point. However, one of his professors drove him in the middle of the night, across state lines, to take the ACT. This moment meant everything to him, and looking back, Jodi pointed out what a difference maker this was, and the sheer amount of gratitude he has for his professor, who was simply expressing his personal appreciation toward Jodi for Jodi's commitment to excellence.

Thus, the common pattern emerges. If you put your time, energy, and mind into something someone cares about, it is a form of appreciation. This appreciation inspires gratitude, and gratitude, when acted upon, appreciation. The cycle then continues and, with high frequencies, a relationship of A-team quality, like this one, will form.

Jodi went through this program, and upon his release, transferred to Stanford University. With this move, he was assigned a new parole officer, who is incredibly understanding of his situation.

"She is very much of the opinion that 'I do not want to stand in your way. Achieve whatever greatness you can, and make your destiny a reality,'" Jodi notes about his relationship with the new officer.

Instead of forcing extra state program training for him, she allows him to spend time in the library, attending seminars, and living his full life as an academic. "She knows I'm a nerd, and my goal isn't to do anything that could get her in trouble. It's more about me learning as much as I can, and she allows me to do that."

"She's really proud of me, and I work hard to make her prouder," he said with a smile.

What Jodi feels is not uncommon. Studies have shown the parolees who have a positive relationship with their parole officer are less likely to commit another crime (Chamberlain Alyssa et al., 2018). This is due to the social support a parole officer can provide, which can literally change our genetic and environmental vulnerabilities and help us become more resilient to stress (Ozbay Fatih et al., 2007). That means having someone who understands and supports you allows you to better respond to the world around you.

Your A-team will understand your struggles, and help you push past them, rather than disqualify your presence because of them. Choose your A-team wisely. It will determine if you're on your A-game or your F-game.

What will you do with the knowledge you can change someone's life for the better by showing them a hint of kindness, by being patient, or acting with humility?

The essence of understanding is you don't need to go out of your way to do it. It just takes a conscious thought. Am I going to be purposeful with my words and non-verbal cues? Will I remove myself from my bubble to learn more about the world and take on the positive emotions that come with eliminating biases? Will I be flexible?

All of these are questions to ponder as you continue about your day. Start now.

TL;DR

Everyone can experience the joy and blessing of generosity; because everyone has something to give.

—JAN GRACE

The three elements to generosity are gratitude, action which inspires appreciation, and understanding toward all.

- Be grateful for everything you are given. Random acts of kindness are one avenue to a happier and more fulfilled life. Think Mother Theresa.
- Find a way to do things for other people that they will appreciate. A change in perspective is sometimes a necessary evil. If this is very difficult, think, "What can I do for this person right now to help me in the future?"
- Be understanding and kind to those around you. You do not know what they are going through, and you are no better than them. Treat all as equals. Act with humility and remember the world does not revolve around you.

PART 2
COURAGE

Courage (noun): the ability to do something that frightens one.

TAKE RISKS

A ship in port is safe; but that is not what ships are built for.

—ALBERT EINSTEIN

The college application process in the United States is highly daunting for many. Seniors are encouraged to apply to six to eight schools, two to three of which are "safeties," meaning almost guaranteed admission based on your grades and exams, four are "targets," and two to three are "reaches," indicating it is unlikely you will get in because admission is highly competitive for this school.

My application process was a complete nightmare. I compiled a list of the top thirty universities in the country (all of which would be labeled "reach" schools) and wrote incredibly generic essays for every single one. In total, there were about a hundred individual prompts and lots of grammatical errors, typos, and nonsensical points in the responses.

For one university in particular, I was feeling incredibly *frisky* and to the prompt of "What song would you say best describes you?" I responded with "I'm Sexy and I Know It." For my response to a longer open-ended prompt of "What motivates you?" I had the brilliant idea of writing about laziness.

To this day, I believe my logic was flawless. Think about it. Carriages, and then the steam engine, were invented so we wouldn't have to walk. Plumbing allowed us to stay within our homes without caring about the world around us. That TV remote buried somewhere in the couch is a technological advancement that was the result of pure human laziness: Who would want to stand up and click buttons on the actual monitor? The cell phone that has your credit card information, contacts, calendar, passwords, alarm clock, calculator, etc. is a creation that epitomizes laziness: You no longer have to remember information, compute calculations, or own physical devices that will take up space. My essay was brilliant. I am lazy, and everything I had done up to that point was to save time or energy.

Simplicity is key. The clearer the message, the better.

My guidance counselor was horrified when she read over my beautifully crafted art. I thought her eyes would pop out of their sockets like slinkies as she was reading over my work. I just sat there, grinning. She strongly recommended I scrap these ideas and rewrite everything immediately.

I did not follow her advice and submitted it anyways. I anxiously awaited an email that would notify me of my admission status. I began to doubt whether I had taken too big of a risk, whether my personality would be overbearing.

The admissions officers must have had brain aneurysms on that particular day when reviewing my file because I was admitted to this particular prestigious university, and I still believe these two particular responses were a stroke of genius. They were *so utterly me.*

My decision to take the riskier path in this specific college application granted me admission to a school many dream of attending. We hear of so many stories of outrageous responses to the questions presented to the eighteen-year-olds eager to start the next journey of their lives. The one thing all college applicants have in common is they are trying to get the admission counselor's attention. How do thousands of bright and like-minded individuals get the attention of a committee of five who have read hundreds of thousands of applications?

It is by being totally and utterly yourself. Being yourself is a risk—it means putting yourself out there for the world to see and judge. If you want to stand out, you need to challenge the status quo. You need to present information in a way that is different, thought-inducing, and inspiring. The expectations of family, friends, coworkers, and society in general can be overwhelming, making us question how our actions fit into the expectations of others. What if you changed your mindset to be "What do I expect out of life?" How would you go about taking that risk, of learning about your strengths and weaknesses, passions and boredoms, habits and perceptions? How would you learn to find comfort in the uncomfortable? Certainly not through following the rules or by being complacent with your expectations. This is because complacency is the enemy of progress.

Taking risks will help you stand out because people generally try to fit in.

This is exactly the mindset Paul Pagnato instills in his employees at PagnatoKarp, a wealth management firm.

Pagnato's greatest asset is his fearless attitude toward standing out. He was previously managing affluent individuals' capital worth about a billion dollars and had also opened up a private banking office in Washington, DC, for the firm. As a manager, he not only had responsibilities to the clients, but also the team, and the company. That is why in 2008, when the financial crisis hit, he was quick to notice conflicts of interest and a lack of transparency which he felt called to fix.

This was an inflection point in his life: he could continue working for a company which he did not find aligning with his values, or he could move on. He came to the conclusion he needed to be an entrepreneur, create disruptive innovation, and this was the only way to address the issues that existed. He chose to take a risk and walked away from the amazing lifestyle he had built up to that point. That marked the founding of PagnatoKarp, which now manages over twelve billion dollars in assets and has ranked number one in Virginia for Forbes Top Wealth

Advisors and number two in Virginia on Barron's Top 1,200 Financial Advisors lists.

At PagnatoKarp, and at other companies though, it was Pagnato's ability to maintain transparent and honest relationships with clients that separated him from the crowd. By doing the right thing, he was taking a risk, and his risks were paying off. He shared a story of another time when taking a big risk ended up paying off, big time.

Someone had just moved to the area, and they wanted to contribute money to a retirement plan, which would cost around $200/month. Pagnato's advice to them was frank, even though it meant Pagnato would be losing out on a potential client: he could open the client an account, but it would be better to go through their employer and establish a 401(k) plan, since this would be pre-tax dollars. They were very grateful and thanked Pagnato for his advice. They went to the company, and it turned out the company did not have a 401(k) plan.

The client returned to Pagnato, referred him to the CEO of the company, and it turned out the company was just getting ready to create a plan. The result: Pagnato ended up getting a profit-sharing plan that had millions of dollars in it. He received the award, a loyal customer, and it all came from staying true to himself and taking a risk.

Embracing change is at the core of how Paul Pagnato operates. He believes change and growth are synonymous, and he thrives on it because, for him, success is failure turned inside out. He thinks about what he expects from himself and from his life, instead of thinking about what was the norm. When speaking to his employee, Oleg Ikhelson, it became apparent this is truly so: The first step for every potential employee is to read a book on exponential organizations, which emphasizes the importance of failure in success, and thus the importance of risk in welcoming change. If the interviewee connects with the topic, then it is likely they will succeed in the work environment presented by Pagnato.

"He expects us to be looking for new ways to do our work, and sometimes it is really hard," Ikhelson points out. "How many ways can you really fill out the taxes? The forms and rules are all the same, but Paul really wants us to get creative and work outside the box." Complacency is not welcome in PagnatoKarp, where progress is expected.

Embracing change is allowing for growth. Stop thinking about the expectations of others for your life and focus on your own.

The thing about complacency is it allows you to settle in, relax, and keep things going at the current status quo. This is best seen in organizations that have suffered from complacency: They lose their competitive edge, top performers, customers, money, and eventually, the business (Ruisi, 2017). Basically, complacency is not the avenue to a self-actualized life. This is because growth of the human psyche, business prosperity, and progress in relationships all require change. The world around us doesn't stop—if we want to be the best version of ourselves, then neither can we.

Buddha came up with three universal truths, two of which focus on change ("Buddhism"). The first states everything is impermanent and changing. The second clarifies this includes the human consciousness. This is supported by modern research in neuroscience, which shows the brain is constantly reorganizing and searching for more efficient connections (Pickersgill, Martin, and Cunningham-Burley, 2015).

Then you may be thinking, why do we become complacent? Why do we think of things as uncomfortable in the first place? Why do they elicit a feeling of fear, similar to our response to danger?

The answer is simple: Danger is the threatened inability to achieve self-actualization. From the very primal definition of self-actualization, on a biological level, self-actualization meant survival (Goldstein, 2000). Animals running around in the wild are faced with anxiety and discomfort at any given moment, but the creation of this discomfort is various threats: another animal eating them, their young being dragged away, or dying from disease. This inborn fear of not surviving is something we have inherited from our ancestors, and we now perceive other things as dangerous: having a low income that is not enough to support our families, not achieving a high enough status that guarantees security, etc. The fear of the unknown has created an evolutionary and instinctive response.

That is why we avoid risk. New environments or situations are ones the brain is not used to. Because the brain seeks to find patterns, once it is able to connect past experiences, processes, and events to their results, it takes less effort. Less effort for the brain makes you more relaxed. This will lead to comfort in a new space.

Herein lies the solution. The more uncomfortable and new situations you come across, the newer connections your brain has the opportunity to make. The more risks you take, the less complacent you allow yourself to be, and thus growth will occur.

> *Consistently putting yourself in uncomfortable situations is the only way to become more comfortable with risk.*

One of the biggest failures in technological advancement lies with Nokia's delayed rollout of a smartphone. Around the late 1990s Nokia had produced two products: one was a colored touch screen with a button on it (what we would now recognize as an early iPhone model) and one was a tablet that would replace a computer, as it had wireless connection and a touch screen (what we would now label an iPad). This was more than seven years before the release of the iPhone, but neither product was ever brought to market (Troianovski and Grundberg, 2012).

The reasoning: Corporate culture did not want to see disruptive innovation hit the market and ruin the exponential success Nokia was seeing in the technology market as the number one phone maker for over a decade. The result: Nokia was ousted from its role, Apple took over the market, and the company is nothing more than a warning story for those falling victim to the siren's call of complacency.

Nokia was thinking about the expectations of the world from them as a company in 1990, rather than thinking about their own expectations for where the company could go and what it could become. This led to them losing their status on top.

Later, when CEO Stephen Elop was speaking to about 2000 Nokia employees, he asked them to raise their hands if they were iPhone users. Few hands went up. His response indicated his personal attitude toward complacency:

"That upsets me—not because some of you are using iPhones, but because only a small number of people are using iPhones. I'd rather people have the intellectual curiosity to understand what we're up against" (Torben, 2021).

It doesn't matter how good you are at something. You need to keep getting better.

This attitude against complacency is something entrepreneurs learn to embody, and in doing so they become open to taking the risks needed to succeed with their endeavors. Erica Rankin, founder of Bro Dough, where she presents a reinvented cookie dough: egg-free, 100 percent vegan, made with heated flour, and high in protein. Her story of complacency with day-to-day life is one that fits our first rule of it hindering progress.

After Rankin graduated from high school, she felt rushed to go to university by her parents, but she was not fully confident about what she wanted to study. After taking a psychology course, which piqued her interest and matched previous endeavors that had caught Rankin's eye, she decided a psychology major would provide the perfect opportunity: It would be the foundation for her to build on. Her thought process: "When I'm done, I can go in any direction."

The next three years, she did just that. She attended classes, worked hard to achieve good grades, but she certainly was not enjoying it. Upon graduation, she began working at another university for about a year and a half, and she was not enjoying this either. The environment was not matching the dynamic she was looking for: There was a traditional nine-to-five schedule with a long commute.

In the time she was working in this mismatched role, she would fill her time by listening to podcasts at her desk. Each day brought something new: business, entrepreneurship, psychology, etc. Every time, Rankin felt an increase of energy, and she was fired up. Filing while sitting at her desk would quickly snap her back to reality, especially when she had to disconnect from the podcast and speak to people on the phone.

Suddenly, an existential crisis hit. Rankin was not getting paid good money; she did not want to do this kind of work anymore. A breaking point in her life had been reached.

"I did not know what I wanted to do with my life. I was living at home, and I felt like a complete loser!"

Rankin's solution: not allowing for complacency to take over. She quit. Up to that point in her life, she had lived in a bubble of a small town with a population of 25,000 people. Everyone knew her, everyone knew her family, and the town's mentality was one of a constant cycle: You start family there, you stay there, you grow old there. No one was contemplating anything other than that. There was no possible future that Rankin could see ahead in that environment. Rankin knew that this simply was not for her. She took her savings, and on a whim, began a backpacking journey through Southeast Asia for about four months.

As she was traveling, she came in contact with the very people she had heard from in her podcasts: entrepreneurs with companies, running their businesses from their laptops, away on vacation, and operating like normal. This was the dream!

"To me, this seemed absolutely fascinating! I never knew I could do this. It got the wheels turning in my head, and I got home from that trip with one thought: 'What can I mix together to create my passion?'" Rankin explained.

As she explored the Canadian market, she realized there was something clearly missing, and it was already a gap she had been filling in her own life, as well as the lives of friends and family: healthy, yummy foods.

When Rankin had competed in bodybuilding competitions, she would take unhealthy recipes and make them healthier. This meant baking protein cakes, protein muffins, protein balls, anything you could imagine. When she shared these recipes online, her followers on Instagram were incredibly receptive.

Now, with the insights she had gained from her travels, and the knowledge she had the opportunity to tap an untouched market, Rankin began her journey: edible, delicious, vegan, high protein cookie dough! Slowly but surely, the company began to grow, and with each new trial or flavor, Rankin constantly worries about the reviews.

"I'm just trying to take the nostalgic feeling I have about cookie dough and make it a constant presence in the lives of those who normally wouldn't touch such a food," she says.

The only way to succeed is to try.

In Rankin's story, if she hadn't dropped her traditional nine to five and had become entirely complacent with the state of affairs in her life, she would still be sitting behind that desk, absolutely miserable, filing paperwork, and listening to podcasts about the type of life she hoped to one day live. But she stepped up. She tried. She could never have foreshadowed her trip to Asia leading to a healthy food business. She found it doesn't matter what kind of risk you take, it's more about how it inspires you.

In her case, she succeeded, but that is not always going to be the case.

The thing about success is that it follows the Universal Rejection Truth: Sometimes you will succeed, and you will do so spectacularly, and sometimes you will fail, which you will also do spectacularly. However, the greater the number of times you try, assuming the success to failure ratio remains the same, the greater the number of times you will succeed. Slowly, it will begin to seem like you are succeeding more, but it is just an increased frequency of trials.

It will be difficult to take risks. Risk-takers are the minority, but truly, it isn't even about loving risk; it is about not being risk averse. Taking calculated risks may include representing an emerging market, being an early adopter of technology, and being yourself instead of fearing the opinions and criticisms of others. Because risks involve uncertainty and change, many people will stay away—but think about it this way: if you don't like something, you have the opportunity to change it. The best way to do so is to change the environment, and thus risk comes into play. Without it, you will guarantee your personal failure. As Mark Zuckerberg said, "The only strategy that is guaranteed to fail is not taking risks" (Desmarais, 2014).

This is something Alex Banayan, author of *The Third Door*, and interviewer of Bill Gates, Maya Angelou, Steve Wozniak, Jane Goodall, Larry King, Jessica Alba, Pitbull,

Tim Ferriss, Quincy Jones, and many more, experienced in his pursuit of these well-known names.

From the very beginning of his journey, Banayan knew what he was looking for: He wanted to get an interview from Bill Gates, an individual whose success had inspired younger Alex to work hard and persevere. In his purpose of finding out what makes successful people successful, Gates fit the characteristic, and Banayan was set on achieving this goal.

Alex Banayan started out just like everyone else, and going into his interview quest, he constantly failed. Rejections came in from left and right, one after the other. Then, one person said yes. They didn't just say yes, though, but rather invited him on a trip to Europe. This trip was about letting go of the expectations he had set for himself, and actually take advantage of the opportunity.

The background behind the trip was unique: This was an absolute stranger who had invited him, and all Banayan had to do was pay for the tickets there. Worst case, he thought to himself, he would lose the money and buy a ticket straight home; best case, he would meet really cool people and learn more about himself (on a free vacation, which never hurts!). The result was better than he could have ever imagined. He learned how to share his story in an engaging way. The first time he told it, the person walked away, completely uninterested because of the way it was presented. So, his mentor brought him up to another person. Then another. Then another. With each new retelling, the story became easier and easier and flowed better. Now, it is the basis of Banayan's plot line for his book, *The Third Door.*

For Banayan, uncomfortable quickly became comfortable, and reaching out and cold calling did too. As he continued to spam people, he would eventually get responses. He lived outside of the expectations that these are unreachable individuals. He lived according to his own rules.

Now, Banayan's book is a *New York Times* bestseller, and it all started from trying. There were infinitely more failures than successes, but the shift in focus and an understanding of the universal rejection truth allowed him to succeed long-term.

Similarly, Shonda Rhimes was incredibly uncomfortable with any form of public speaking. She was incredibly antisocial, fat, and terrified of public speaking. Then she had a life-altering moment when her sister said Rhimes never says yes to anything. That was when Shonda realized "yes" meant uncomfortable, while "no" was now comfortable for her. By sheltering herself from the world around her, she was not experiencing anything new, and even though she was creating through her scripts, she was not *living.* She saw her kids filled with wonder and she knew she had to start saying yes to things.

Up to that point, anything relating to publicity was a no. That included meeting with Jimmy Fallon on "Saturday Night Live." Jimmy Fallon and late-night show experience made her think she was going to puke, but they made accommodations. The interview was shot ahead of time, rather than live. Fallon did most of the talking. Rhimes left not having remembered anything.

But she survived it. So, she said yes to the next thing. Eventually, she spoke to Oprah and remembered it. Now, all those things looking back seem incredibly easy.

Yes, is now easier to say than no, and it is because the uncomfortable became comfortable. Why? Because she tried. She said yes. She allowed herself to fail, choke, and die.

Slowly, these two individuals became more and more successful because they were constantly putting themselves out there, and as they did so, the uncomfortable began to seem comfortable. Even though the stories and the types of risks the individuals were taking were very different, they both took a chance. It is important to step out of your comfort zone in your own capacity.

Get comfortable with the uncomfortable. Do this by living my setting your own expectations.

As children, we are constantly exploring because we have to. We lose this curious mindset because we become risk-averse; we stop questioning things and we stop exploring. We perceive the world differently and maintain a high degree of ability to handle anxiety. We are self-actualizing with each new skill picked up, each new word learned, and each first step taken. Between childhood and adulthood, we develop a tendency to be averse to risk, thus hindering the sheer number of times we try something, due to the fear of failure, and the potential for danger. The result is a lack of self-actualization.

We learn not to bet on ourselves, and that is the worst mistake you could make. If you don't like something, go out and do it yourself. This will test you more than anything because it means only *you* are responsible for your failure. On the flip side, it is also only you who gets to claim the success.

In high school, I was intensely playing piano. I had gone through the Associated Board of the Royal School of Music program, completing eight years of practical piano exams as well as five years of theory exams. With each year, the material would get harder and harder, and the commitment to the instrument meant less time to explore other interests, like the dancing I had done until eighth grade or the gymnastics competitions I enjoyed throughout elementary school.

I decided to pursue an associate degree in piano in sophomore year. This meant putting together an hour-long program to perform in front of the judge, with pieces selected from a long list of approved choices, and at least one representing each of the four time periods. An hour-long program meant up to three hours of daily practice, as well as weekends filled with piano, exhausted fingers, and a cramped wrist. Every week, I had two hours of one-on-one lessons with my piano teacher, who had allowed me to grow into the pianist I am today. Little tweaks in fingering, changes in note connection, and a completely different approach to my usual style became the norm.

Finally, the day came. I walked into the performance hall with a big smile, presented myself to the judge, and sat down in front of the full-sized Steinway. An hour flew by, and I poured my soul into the music coming from my fingers. I stood up, bowed, wished the judge a nice day, and left the room.

Now, it was a waiting game. Weeks would pass before I heard back from the ABRSM organization about my degree, but around late July, I finally got the giant envelope. It was this moment that would make it or break it.

My score: 32/50.

The score required to pass: 33/50.

The judge's comment: Well done. Work on it.

At this moment, I declared to my family I was done, and piano was a thought of the past. There would be no more piano playing in the future, and I certainly would never be working with the ABRSM again, much less with my teacher. My mom took this surprisingly well, given that she generally pushes me endlessly. As the leader of my A-team, she knows exactly when I am not committing myself fully to something, but she had been home when I was practicing. She knew I had left it all in the performance room that day. She did not say anything to me.

Around October, she brought up the possibility of trying again. My immediate response: no. Absolutely not. I was in my junior year of high school, taking undergraduate classes in my free time, tutoring for tens of hours a week, and I was directing the school musical. Piano was not part of that equation.

"Think about it. You would do it alone this time. Just try. Worst case, you become a better pianist. Best case, you walk away with a diploma," she said.

Yeah, and I walk away with hundreds of wasted hours, I thought, rolled my eyes, and went back to bed.

The deadline to sign up for the exam was fast-approaching, as forms were generally due in early November. Normally, I would start practicing in August, have everything filled out as soon as possible, and be in performance mode by April. April and May were my final push, with extra time and energy spent at the bench. This year was different. If I even said yes, I would be starting in November. The test date had been pushed up to late March. In piano land, that was next week.

To my mother's surprise, I agreed. The next few months were terrible. I would switch between YouTube and different versions of the sheet music to see how different people had annotated the notes. Days were filled with listening to three-second nuances over and over on repeat so I could replicate them exactly on my instrument. Suddenly, March was here. Mid-March was here. Late March had me knocking on the performance hall door, entering, sitting down at the bench, and passing out for an hour, once again leaving me with no recollection of my performance. I left the judge with a smile and waited again for the news for several weeks.

Once again, the envelope arrived. This time, it was all on me. It was my score, not a reflection of my teacher's. If I had failed once again, the issue was *me*.

My score: 44/50.

I had done it. I had listened to all the advice given to me over the last decade of my piano, heard it, and then done it. It was uncomfortable. It was scary. What was scarier was I had done it myself. I did not have to share that accomplishment with my teacher. It was *all* me.

> *The biggest and most rewarding risk you can take is betting on yourself.*

This is the ultimate lesson of taking risks: Be simple with your messaging, stay true to yourself, avoid complacency, and bet on yourself. Risks will allow you to prosper in a world that strives to be complacent and blend in. As blasé as it sounds, *you* can do it.

NEVER ASSUME

Assumptions are made, and most assumptions are wrong.

—ALBERT EINSTEIN

Have you ever had an open conversation with someone that made you realize many of your worries were in your head? Or avoided participating in an activity because of a thought that was never confirmed by anyone else? Maybe the thought was you weren't welcome, or you would be interrupting? Maybe it's too late since it's already started? This type of thinking, where we take assumptions as facts, is something I struggle with.

It was in eighth grade my geometry teacher drilled in a very important lesson: never assume.

My teacher, Mrs. Murti, called on me to solve a question on the board. Now, for some background on my mathematical skills, math is not something I had ever struggled with. All the women on my mom's side of the family are math teachers and professors, so I grew up around math. Equations, exponents, logic puzzles—it was all fine. Geometry was not.

Geometry and I were not friends. Sitting and staring at the "Given:..." and "Prove:..." was my biggest nightmare. Being called on to go through a proof *on my own* would normally exhilarate me, but because it was Geometry class, it was terrifying. I started with the steps I have been taught: Rewrite the given, never assume, think about the possible rules that could be used. My brain was having a big "Uh..." moment.

Ah! These two sides look the same, so this is why the proof works. I ended the problem and sat back down. Apparently, this was not the case because the figure was not drawn to scale. I was not allowed to assume anything about the lengths of the sides, and this made my solution invalid. Just because the sides *seemed* the same did not mean they were. The lesson I left that class with has stuck with me since then.

Even though she was referring to the shapes drawn on the page in front of me, for which I had to write multi-step proofs, my teacher made a widely applicable point.

Just because something seems a certain way does not mean it is. Avoid making up explanations in your head.

I tried solving the proof again, this time in twenty-seven steps, and showed it to my teacher. She smirked, and said, "Ester, when people want to touch their nose, they pick up their hand and put their pointer finger to the tip of their nose. When you logic through something," and then she took her arm and wrapped it around her head, "You do it like this," and made a full circle back to her nose. She smiled. "Well done, but it is a three-step proof, just so you know."

My relationship with this teacher showed me even if I did not think I could solve the proof, or it was taking forever, I should not assume I can't do it. I should keep trying. Those absolutely awful problems knocked me down to a humbler state, where I went into the exam knowing it doesn't matter what the shape looks like, or even if I measure the angle or length to get a ratio—I can never assume.

This mentality of avoiding assumptions opens up the world: It allows people to be truly themselves around you. It allows you to avoid creating nonexistent explanations.

For some people, not making assumptions is the only way to get what you want. It is about recognizing if you don't ask, the answer is already "no," and that the worst-case scenario if you do ask is "no." Even though this may not be the answer you want to hear, at least it is one you did not create in your mind.

Chuck Offenburger's story of acquiring black and white saddle shoes proves avoiding making assumptions is the only way to live life to the fullest.

When his older brother came home from the University of Iowa back in the mid 1950s, he was wearing black and white saddle shoes, and Chuck instantly fell in love. They were the coolest thing he had ever seen, so he ordered them from the G.H. Bass Shoe Company, and they became the only shoes he would ever wear.

"They've got the perfect orange crepe soul and they're lightweight. They're really skippy looking and I realize you, Ester, and 98 percent of Americans think they look dorky, but I don't give a damn," he told me after showing me his pair, and continued telling the story.

In 1994, he stopped by a little shoe shop where a woman named Linda Hart would regularly fix his shoes. She looked at the shoes he handed her and shook her head.

"I'm not fixing those one more time," she said.

"What do you mean?"

"I've already re-soled those shoes three times. They're shot. Go get new ones," she told him, so he went to the local G. H. Bass outlet in search of a pair of men's black and white saddle shoes. They told him they did not have them, and they were not in the catalog, either. Offenburger was connected to the Customer Service Hotline, which he called as soon as he returned home, getting Linda Wood on the phone.

"I'd like to order a pair of men's size 10.5 black and white saddle shoes," he requested.

"We don't have those anymore," she responded.

"Why not?"

"Well, there's no demand," she explained.

"Well, there is in Iowa," he pointed out.

"We haven't noticed."

"Okay, listen, I know this would cost me an arm and a leg... but how much would it cost to special-make me a pair?"

"Mr. Offenburger, this is the G.H. Bass Shoe Company. We are the largest retail shoe company in the world. We don't special-make a pair of shoes for anybody," was the answer. Chuck pushed further, asking how many orders from his friends it would take for them to consider making the shoes. "No offense, but you just don't have that many friends," Linda told him, marking the end of the conversation.

At this point, it would have been easy to give up. No shoes, no problem. There are thousands of other possibilities, and shoes really don't make that much of a difference. It is easy to assume there are no other possibilities, that this is the end of the decades-long time of Chuck's relationship with the black and white saddle shoe.

A possible assumption is that there are no possibilities. This is rarely the case. Keep pushing.

Chuck kept pushing. He was a columnist for the *Des Moines Register* at the time, so he immediately wrote a column. "I'm one of six known adult male wearers of black and white saddle shoes in Iowa, and I named the others. All our shoes are worn out. We know how much the rest of you have been watching us wear these shoes and thinking how cool we look in them, and how you've always wanted a pair. So now is your time to step up. Write me letters or send them into the Register about why you think the Bass Shoe Company should do this," he summarized. About twenty-five letters came in, prompting Chuck to write another column. This time about seventy-five letters came in, one of which noted the movie *Bridges of Madison County* starring Clint Eastwood that was being filmed right then in Iowa. The author of the letter recommended Chuck get Clint Eastwood to wear a pair of these shoes in the movie so all of America would want them.

Chuck wrote this up in a column and faxed excerpts of the letters to the G.H. Bass Shoe Company customer service location in South Portland, Maine.

About two days later, he received a letter from the G.H. Bass Shoe Company's G. Mitchell Massey, senior vice president of retail, had written to him. He told Chuck it was not necessary to get Clint Eastwood to put on a pair of these shoes for the movie. They would surrender. Massey gave Chuck the opportunity to put in an order—sixty-five dollars for men's shoes, $62.50 for women's. "He told me to buy two pairs myself, since this wouldn't happen again," Chuck noted.

Chuck wrote another article, which resulted in an order of 658 pairs of black and white saddle shoes, and a total of $48,600. The president of Bass Shoes went into orbit;

he just couldn't believe it! He was running around the factory, making sure everyone knew the shoes had to be done in time for the Iowans to wear them to Christmas church services. They retooled the factory and began working! Within a few days, Bass had its sales force wear the first ten pair of saddle shoes produced to the New York City Shoe Show, the biggest shoe show in the world, resulting in ten thousand orders for the saddle shoes. The people of Iowa received their shoes in time for Christmas.

The kicker: Chuck was featured on page one of the fashion section of the *New York Times*, which he said was "the high point of my whole journalism career!" What was a simple push toward what Chuck initially wanted became more. He was being recognized on a national level for the work he had done in avoiding assumptions and in continuing to keep going toward his goal. In this journey, he had self-actualized. He had been courageous in asking questions and avoiding assumptions, authentic in his mission to have the shoes he desired, and generous with people's time in the process.

Avoid assuming you deserve anything less than what you desire. Even if you don't get exactly what you were looking for, other doors will open in the process.

What if Chuck had assumed the G.H. Bass Shoe Company would not have these shoes, and never gone to the outlet? What if he had chosen to accept the very first no as fact? What if he not written those columns? These what-if scenarios can haunt you, especially if you assume that how things seem is how they are.

This line of thinking is the mentality Matthew Henry had when putting together his third book. For him, the element of avoiding assumption meant something different. It meant allowing himself to be curious and explore all the elements of his various interests, and ask questions outside of the fields he was an expert in. The first book, titled *Working Together: Why We Need Bipartisanship in American Politics*, explored the role of empathy in the modern political world. The second book, titled *Dating Yourself: Finding Self-Love Before True Love*, explores the importance of finding a connection with oneself before continuing to connect with anyone else in an intimate manner. The third book, which he is currently writing, discusses the stock market and how to build capital.

As you can probably tell, all three books have incredibly different themes and storylines, impacts on the world, and require different approaches to fully putting together a project as large as a published piece of work. Henry's mentality throughout each journey was simple: Ask questions. Keep asking questions. He had been interested in politics and was able to communicate well enough with various different types of people to allow him to grow to understand that at the core, everyone just wants the best for themselves and their families but hopes to accomplish that in different ways. He asked the important question: Why? Why do we have so much political discourse? Why is the US more racially divided than ever before? Why are people unwilling to compromise? Going into each conversation, Henry had one rule: Leave any assumptions at the door. It did not matter what his personal political opinion was, because the goal was to come to an agreement, not end with an argument. And he was successful.

With the second book, Henry's journey was sparked by his own personal struggle with depression. He recognizes the fact there are more resources available today to those with poor mental health, but he offers a note of caution: we cannot assume there will be a continued emphasis on mental health in twenty, fifty, or a hundred years. He once again found his role as the communicator through his writing, by avoiding assuming anything about anyone about any time anywhere. The results were magical. His book sales soared.

Henry summarized his mentality this way: "I never assume I am the smartest one in the room. Instead, I look for the smartest ones in the room, and I learn from them. As I started talking to more and more successful people, they all had one thing in common: They asked questions and they read books. So, I started reading books. I'm not doing anything new or crazy, but I am staying in a constant mode of success. My success won't come when I reach my goal; I am already there, and with each goal, my success grows."

The ability to maintain a global view, and avoid stagnation has allowed Henry to prosper, speaking for TEDx and connecting with mentors consistently. He asks questions, avoids assumptions, and does not set expectations. Rather, he stated, "I do not believe in limits. I do not believe in fairness. There is only working hard, becoming a better person, and building on accomplishments."

> *The one assumption you're allowed to make: You are never the smartest person in the room. You can always learn from someone.*

When you make assumptions, you are coming up with your own reasoning for something that has nothing to do with you. This is exactly what happened in my world history class with Mr. Jeffrey Martin. When I walked into the class on the first day of freshman year of high school, it was also his first day ever teaching. He warned us the entire year would be a learning experience, and it truly was. There was one particular assignment that discussed elements of a religious text with a modern analysis of misconceptions, responding to a prompt he had presented that I did not personally agree with.

The assignment was clear: Explain how the text disproves a common misconception.

Instead of clarifying the details of the assignment with him, I wrote an entire research paper proving the misconception is actually fact. I spent several days putting the elements of my paper together, creating a detailed outline, and reading the entirety of the religious text. I then wrote the paper that was originally requested, stapled the two together, and turned them in. That is, I wrote two full papers, one per the requirements, and the other was an explanation of why this was a biased and unfounded assignment.

> Communicating your thoughts will help clarify assumptions.

I was incredibly anxious when Mr. Martin returned my paper. He left a comment at the top of the extra work I had done that said something along the lines of, "You should have just talked to me about it." After class, I explained I had not only assumed he wouldn't be receptive to me writing a different paper, but also that he would not have been receptive to me not writing a paper for the requested topic. The result ended up being double the work on my part and double the work on his part. Had I not assumed, everything would have been much easier for us both.

When I spoke to Mr. Martin after graduation, specifically for an interview for the book, he told me something very interesting. From a very young age, people had assumed he was not incredibly intelligent, but it was more a lack of application in school because of turmoil at home that had led to bad grades. "I learned very early on I can't lean on what I've experienced to model what someone should learn from me," Martin said. Growing up, he had been a child that did not need to be disciplined because he never really did bad things; he never got in trouble and did not get involved in drugs or alcohol.

As Martin's student for three years, I genuinely did not expect that type of response from my former teacher. He had always been relaxed in class, allowing students to drive discussions, up to date on current events, and ready to discuss the new rap releases. The idea of Mr. Martin only discovering alcohol at twenty-five years old was fascinating to me. *An assumption on my part.*

"I'm the polar opposite of that in reality. I look at it as you need to represent the values you would want someone to learn from you. Those are the core things, which for [Martin] are empathy, honesty, transparency...," he says. "Our country and our world would get a lot further if everyone just stopped and thought about what things look like from someone else's side of the aisle."

This mentality has allowed Martin to be incredibly successful in creating connections with students. Going into the classroom is exciting for him because of the pressure on lifelong learning that exists. He never knows what the day will look like, and Martin never hesitates to spend five minutes talking about a personal experience or allowing a student to do the same. "When I walk into the classroom, there are eighteen to thirty question marks. When you put so many question marks into one room, there is absolutely no way to predict what will happen, regardless of how much time I put into the lesson plan. I need to adapt, and I can't be complacent."

Mr. Martin is the type of teacher to make bird noises to get the class to calm down. He is also the teacher I went to discuss my college decision with, in terms of where to apply and where to end up attending. He *never assumes* anything about a student's background, intellect, abilities, or personal story. If we chose to share, he was there to listen. If not, his class was a wild time, and we certainly learned the material.

In Martin's life, there were a lot of assumptions he experienced toward himself growing up, so he chooses not to do the same toward others. A person who never assumes is the type of person you want on your A-team.

People who you can trust to communicate with you, rather than making assumptions about you, are who you want on your A-team.

In the journey of writing this book, I slowly started to put together a list of the incredibly important people I wanted to speak to. There were so many assumptions that came with that:

1) I was assuming they are important. Who is important, anyways? Maybe these are individuals who have in some way impacted my life, but would their stories have the same impact on others?
2) I was assuming they would be unreachable. My bubble burst on that one. Everyone is reachable as long as you ask the right way, at the right time, and through the right person.
3) Even if I could reach them, would they respond? Probably not, so why email them anyway?
4) Let's say they respond. I get to talk to someone amazing. What do I ask? How do I build a connection? How do I maintain that relationship?

Great logic, right? Especially when I was speaking to individuals who are friends with the Obama family, the Trump family, world-renowned researchers, authors, and speakers.

This logic of a quick one, two, three, four is unlike me. My go-to is send the email/text/voice message and move on. For some reason, though, it was not happening with reaching out on behalf of the book. I was assuming there would be no answer, or the answer would be "no." It was not until I met someone at an event who heard about my goal of reaching Michelle Obama, sent me a list of contact emails, phone numbers, and addresses, reached out to these people on my behalf, and then saw me again a week later and was incredibly disappointed to find out I had not reached out that I finally took my leap of faith. I sent the emails! "Now we wait," I thought. In the meantime, I started reaching out to other influential people who had been on my list.

That night, I got a LinkedIn request from Michelle Obama's friend: "Hi Ester, I am excited to read your book."

The next morning an email from Airbnb co-founder and CTO, as well as chairman of Airbnb China, Nate Blecharczyk made my day.

I had assumed the answer would be no, but I had not even asked. What if I had asked months ago?

Making poor assumptions sets you up for failure. Approach things with an open mind.

Amy Morin, an international bestselling author and psychotherapist, discusses the role of fairness and her personal assumptions about life in her TEDx Talk, "The Secret of Becoming Mentally Strong," where expectations resulted in complete desolation for a long period of time. She breaks down what mentally strong people don't do into three categories: Assume bad things happen to them, hold unhealthy beliefs about others, and unhealthy beliefs about the world.

In the context of making assumptions, when you assume bad things are going to happen to you, you are focused on the problem, not the solution. As Morin puts it, while you are busy throwing yourself a pity party, you could be taking steps to make someone else's life better. When you hold unhealthy beliefs about others, you are giving them the power. If you are assuming someone wants to do something to hurt you, you are the one feeling paranoid, stressed, tense, and putting the situation entirely in their hands.

Morin explains there are very few things you truly *have* to do. No one can *drive you crazy* unless you let them. It is up to you. Do not assume something is mandatory. Set your own rules, boundaries, and expectations. Finally, Morin emphasizes unhealthy beliefs about the world, in the sense that the world owes you something, is critical to poor mental health long term. For instance, with this belief, if you go into an interview having prepared and worked incredibly hard, and then were not hired, you would be devastated.

A basic example of this is even buckling your seatbelt. We've all experienced that frustrating day when everything is going wrong. You're sitting in the car, trying to get the seatbelt in without looking. It keeps missing, and your frustration only increases with each failed attempt. "Gosh, this is just never going to work!" you think to yourself. This is not the mindset to have. Instead, think "Almost there!" because the mindset change is an invitation to be patient with yourself. Changing your mindset can have significant positive results.

In Morin's personal life, she experienced alignment in her finances, relationship, and career very early on. As a twenty-three-year-old, she had just finished graduate school, been hired as a therapist, gotten married, and bought a big house. Then, she got a call from her sister. Her mother was unresponsive; the woman who woke up every morning happy to be alive soon passed away from a brain aneurysm, despite having no history of health problems. On the three-year anniversary of Morin's mother's passing, her husband collapsed on the floor. Morin was mortified, called an ambulance and her husband's family, and that night the doctor informed her that her spouse had passed from a heart attack. He was twenty-six years old and had no history of heart problems. A few years later, Morin got married again, and almost immediately her new husband's father was diagnosed with a terminal illness and passed way within the year.

For Morin, assuming the world is fair was not an option. This assumption would mean taking on the belief she deserved the death that was happening around her and the people who were suffering were doing so because of her. Even more so, it would mean she would be stuck in the past, reliving the grief from each death. Instead, she had to be mentally strong and give up the destructive mental habits.

For her, it meant getting off social media because she began to assume the highly edited selected posts were the norm. It meant stopping the constant comparisons to others and catching herself when she was degrading herself in her mind.

Morin was mentally strong. She gave up the mental habits that would be destructive; chief among them was the assumption the world is a fair place. She realized it is only our own choices that hold us back. Other people are separate from us, and we cannot assume anything about anyone, including ourselves. We cannot hold ourselves to other people's standards and can compare ourselves solely to the person we were the day before.

Believe in the power of your mind.

In Morin's life, assuming would have been lethal. It would have wracked her emotional wellbeing and destroyed her mental health. For others, like Matthew Henry, leaving any and all assumptions at the door has allowed him to expand his expertise and grow into a lifelong learner. I have stopped assuming the answer will be "no." What assumptions will you quit making? How will you become mentally stronger?

Remember to tough it out through bad times you need to know your world is what you make it. Before you can change it, you need to believe you can, and you definitely cannot do that if you assume it is impossible to do so. The Vanderbilt Rebbetzin told me the following, and since then, it has been at the back of my mind at all times: When you meet someone, accept them. Accept them fully. Love them, and do not place any expectations. They will not only flower in your presence and want to be around you more, but they will grow into a mold that works for you both. They will give you what you give them.

In your acceptance of others, never assume, and ask questions.

EXPLORE WITHOUT LIMITS

We shall not cease from exploration, and the end of all our exploring will be to arrive where we started and know the place for the first time.

—T. S. ELIOT

I have always resonated with the character of Dora the Explorer. Even though I found the show itself wildly unamusing as a child, I have never been afraid to push boundaries. But I did so differently than the typical rebellious child, so my parents and teachers were supportive of my adventures. The goal in school was to finish my work as fast as possible. Racing through the math problems or the assigned science worksheet meant I could get to what I truly wanted to do: read. I pushed myself each and every day to go faster. Turning in the quiz early meant an extra twenty minutes of freedom, silence to enjoy consuming the words on the pages in front of me. Completing a group project within a fourth of the allotted time meant I could use the school computer to research my new fascination. I was *the* explorer, in my mind.

Exploration takes on virtually every possible form: physical, mental, emotional, spiritual. Anything you have perceived up to this point in your life has been a reflection of your current views because our emotions influence our memories and greatly impact how we interact with our environment. Ultimately, exploration comes down to one simple fact: Life is not a ladder. There is no guided next step, no straight edge to keep you within the lines; there is no safety net at the bottom if you fall. Rather, it is a beautiful spiral, rollercoaster-like in the sense it changes altitude and warps into whatever new future you create. With that in mind, there is virtually no way to land in the same location in the same way ever again on that journey, just like it is impossible to do so in your life.

You can explore even what seems normal. Change your perspective.

Stephen Box has always thought outside the lines. He describes himself as an accidental activist and a community choreographer. No matter the description you may assign him, he certainly explores past the written lines and takes advantage of any opportunity presented to him.

Box grew up with driven parents. They had graduate degrees from Australia and had come to the US to continue their education, and Box followed in their footsteps by pursuing an undergraduate degree. Upon beginning, he received the advice, "Don't worry, you will figure out what you want to be." Next year, it never came. The following year, Box was still clueless. Somehow, a biology major had come about from Box's love for science, math, rules, and puzzles, but it wasn't something Box saw himself pursuing long term. Rather, he made an opportunity out of every situation he encountered.

This became particularly apparent when Box began to describe his involvement in a Hollywood film production. One morning, he was riding his bicycle in San Gabriel Valley, and he rode up into the mountains. Later in the day, coming back down the one-way street in the small little town of Glendora, he rode right into a movie set. The street had been closed off to shoot the film at the end of traffic, but they had not anticipated anyone being on the other end—except for Stephen Box. So, he rode right into the set, right down into the heart of movie production, and immediately began making friends.

Quickly, Box began to interact with the people around him. Through chatting, he had begun to recognize names and faces, and when it came time for a company move, it was Box who made things possible. The producer of the movie needed the transportation captain to relocate the trucks because nothing could happen without the transportation caption approval. No one knew his name, though. What a dilemma! Instead of finding out his names, the producers and actors were yelling at the transportation captain (not an ideal way to get someone to do something, much less so in a stressful situation).

"Hey, Charlie, can you do me a favor? Can you give me a stake bed and send it over here?" he asked, and the transportation captain immediately obliged. Box remembered his name, making the interaction even more personal.

It turned out this had been the first day of shooting, and everyone was so busy figuring out their own situation they were completely disregarding everyone else. Everyone was desperate to make a lasting positive impression on those around them, but no one took the time to learn names, smile, or smoothen the process. Box did this, expressed care for each new person he met, and learned that truly anything was possible. Nothing was off limits for him, as long as he was kind and put in the effort to get acquainted with everyone. In the years that came, Box made it his job to explore every possible way to make things move more smoothly.

> *Caring about the people around you will help you get the lay of the land faster (and get you opportunities you didn't know were available.*

That meant the skills he had learned working in restaurants and nightclubs, gathering people skills and increasing his organizational efficiency. When I asked if he had any experience working on set, his response was simple: "Well, yes, I know what people are."

At the end of the day, Box's exploration has always been, and will always be, about people. That first day showed he was more than capable of interacting positively with those around him, and he was asked to stay on set. He was there as an assistant producer, with the role of getting everyone to the finish line, and ahead of scheduling, under budget. In many cases, that meant catering to the crew's needs outside of what was expected. He paid attention to what brand of cigarettes they smoked, and he would purchase all those brands. At midnight, when the crew would run out of cigarettes, they would want to leave, and Box became the one to trust because everyone knew he could be counted on for whatever could possibly come up.

In Box's life, exploration to the highest degree has allowed him to entertain such opportunities. He pushed past what is expected and doesn't set limitations. With his children, he is a fun-schooler, similar to homeschooling, but guided by the students. With his work in the government, he started out as a property developer, and turned his mission into helping the homeless by providing his personal assets to make lasting impact.

When the producer of the movie wanted to impress Randy Travis, and proposed the idea of throwing a barbecue, he turned to Box. Box was quick to point out the dietary restrictions the singer-songwriter has that would make this less than ideal of a scenario. The reason why Box knew this? He observed, explored, and left extra space on his calendar. For him, it was never about having the map because he was aware unfolding it in one place won't help if it is a map for the wrong place.

Observe what is going on around you and then make time for what needs to be done in your calendar (and space in your mind).

The beautiful thing about goals is once you set your mind to something, you can achieve it. Within reason, nothing is impossible. However, certain limitations come with that. For instance, it would be entirely possible for me to sit down and write this book in ninety days. Every single day for the first two weeks, I would read a book and put together a summary. The following two weeks, I would conduct back-to-back interviews. The following month, every two days, I would write a chapter and then spend the last month editing. It would be intense. It would be crazy. The reason why? Sacrifice. Pumping out a book in ninety days would mean seeing less of my family, not interacting with my friends, not learning about other topics I am interested in, and producing a product entirely in line with the initial vision. But what about the second or third vision? The small idea I started exploring halfway through became a reality that never would have been an option.

Think about the most exciting, rewarding, or emotional moment in your life. Write it down.

_____

_____

_____

Did you plan it? How did it occur? If you did plan it, was it something that went according to plan? If so, was this the very original plan you had?

_____

_____

_____

When Steve Wozniak was putting together the computer, it was all about exploration and not at all about a goal. There was no urgency, but rather an enormous relief in a lack of focus. His questions were all over the place: What is an engineer? What is a computer? How could he take it apart and reassemble it to improve productivity? All of this led to what we now know as the Apple.

The most important discoveries are often by accident. Think about the discovery of penicillin: Alexander Fleming forgot to cover his sandwich!

Paul Gurney found the importance of exploration in his life as he discovered the world. Having grown up in a little town in England called Torquay, there was never much particularly exciting happening. Neither of Gurney's parents had gone to pursue a formal education through college, and at his own school there was no real environment of ambition or high achievement. Rather, these were rarely discussed. As a result, Gurney never even considered he could personally achieve some of the things he had seen on TV. It was not a conscious thought of being unable to achieve things, but rather that it was just so out of the realms of possibility there was no reason for Gurney to even consider them in the first place.

Gurney ended up going to a top university, not due to some profound drive to study, but rather because it seemed like something he should do. When he did, his eyes were opened to more possibilities of what the world could offer. He finished his degree with high honors. Despite only ever having been on a plane twice, he then spent a year traveling, something he was inspired to do from watching TV as a kid.

Gurney then went back to school to get a master's degree after being offered a full scholarship to return. What a change of pace—going from the unimaginable to having a spot paid for him. After some time lecturing and another year of travel, Gurney was hired by Accenture, a big global consulting company. At twenty-four years old, Gurney started work full-time.

Something was nudging him to do more, though. He set up a fundraising initiative to send Accenture employees to Kilimanjaro, the highest mountain in Africa. Immediately, the negative comments started to flow in: "You don't have any experience," "You have never raised any money before," "You aren't senior enough to organize this."

A year later, Gurney was at the top of the mountain with twenty-four colleagues, having collectively raised a quarter of a million dollars. The next year, he organized six trips and raised over a million dollars. He started doing higher mountains and more ambitious and adventurous things. A few years later, Gurney found himself doing the two toughest races on earth back-to-back, a 400-mile race to the North Pole and then 160-mile run across the Sahara Desert. These were all things he should never have been able to do. If he had believed what people were saying about his ability to achieve these things, he would still be sitting behind a desk wondering what was possible and believing he had achieved his potential.

> *Exploration will give you perspective. If you set your mind to it, truly anything is possible.*

Today, Gurney is the co-founder of BecomingX, an organization that aims to redefine success and create a world where everyone can realize their potential. He has interviewed almost one hundred of the world's most inspiring people, recording over a million words in conversation, and highlights interviews with Roger Federer, Courteney Cox, Channing Tatum, Julia Roberts, world record-setting athletes, and some of the most recognizable names in business and politics. His physical exploration led him to a mental one, and now he is on a journey of learning more about what success means to him and sharing the lessons he has learned over the years with the younger generations of today. For Gurney, no limits existed. He explored without boundaries.

This limitless exploration can only happen without urgency. We seek urgency because it brings us comfort: If we figure things out right now, we will not have to do so later. It helps us cope with the unknown, but the truth is simple. There is no urgency, and it is imperative to find relief in a lack of focus. This can come through exploration, and more importantly, through constant curiosity. What lies beyond your current personal physical boundaries? Your mental ones? Think big and set the universe as your box.

Dick Bay found himself through constant exploration. There were many careers, many teams, and many, many, many changes. In high school, Bay took a humanities course that he cites as one of the most influential in his life, leading him to think and perceive differently. It covered philosophy, religion, world history, art, music, and combined all of Bay's hobbies and interests into one. This got him hooked on philosophy, and he decided to go in that direction for the undergraduate career: a major in philosophy and minors in English and religion. Long term, this course had also exposed Bay to Buddhism, and he is now a practicing Buddhist.

When Bay entered his senior year at Vanderbilt, his intention at that point was to go on to graduate school and become a philosophy professor. But one day, something prompted a walk down 21st Avenue, where he experienced an epiphany. There was a moment of inspiration where Bay decided he really wanted to pursue something more creative than being a professor, but what that may be, he had no clue. It was time to explore. He had done some student films, but then a close friend set him up to play music at the Vanderbilt Graduate Student Pub. There, he met a professional guitar player, they hit things off, and until his thirties, Bay was in the music business.

> *Sometimes, you have to go through a few different paths to find the right one. It's all part of the journey.*

A decade working in music occasioned much satisfaction for Bay, but it failed to pay the bills. When he turned thirty, he decided he needed a more stable career. Without knowing what that career might be, his short-term solution was temping, and that ended up leading to the long-term solution. Luckily, he was placed at a company where he got along exceptionally well with everyone, and eventually he was transferred to the accounting department. As he was working, Bay noticed something. There was a Radio Shack computer standing in the corner gathering dust. A former vice president of the firm had brought the computer, no one was using it, and it just stared at Bay each and every day. Although Bay had absolutely no experience relating to computers, he got the notion the computer could do aspects of his job better than he could do manually.

One day, on a whim, Bay went out and bought a book on how to program (this was in the '80s). This quickly opened up a career path that had never been there before, one he never would have even imagined or foreseen, and he stayed with that. He was never particularly ambitious about this new path, but it did allow him to quickly climb the corporate ladder, and he found new ways to be creative with programming.

"I had a friend who became a computer programmer after graduation, and I thought that just sounded horrible to me! Once I got into it, I found it was incredibly creative and satisfying," Bay recounts. During his corporate career, he taught himself how to play jazz piano, and since retiring, he has returned to the music world.

There are many things to take away from Dick Bay's life story.

1) Opportunities are everywhere, you just need to take them. You can't take them if you don't know they exist. You find out they exist by exploring. For Dick Bay, this started with opening his mind up to the information being given to him in the context of the humanities class. It continued with his push into the music world and his opportunity to play at the Pub. Finally, it meant looking at the computer and doing something about it.
2) You need to act. If you are out and about exploring, act on your intuition. Dick Bay went out and followed his hunch of programming. This was something completely new to him, and nothing he had proper training in ever before. Instead of shying away from the challenge, he took it upon himself to learn and encouraged himself to keep going.
3) Nothing is off limits. No one was standing over Bay's shoulder and telling him to pursue philosophy. Likewise, no one was encouraging him to go into music. No one asked Bay to take a look at the computer, or even dust it off. It is all about initiative, and if the initiative is there at the right time during exploration, then anything is a real possibility.
4) Everything is new at first. When you are exploring your surroundings for the first time, it can feel odd because it is new information being processed. With time, practice, and consistency, even the act of exploration becomes easier to manage. Limits fall away, and even "new" can become "old." Age is just a number!

Explore without defining barriers for yourself.

Having the courage to explore makes the world of a difference. There are many ways to do this, but it comes from a yearning for a difference in perspective. Explore the normal world without biases and make time for constant exploration. Do so with an open mind without self-set restrictions. Who knows what you'll discover in the process? Maybe your purpose and mission in life!

TL;DR

I learned that courage was not the absence of fear, but the triumph over it. I felt fear myself more times than I can remember, but I hid it behind a mask of boldness. The brave man is not he who does not feel afraid, but he who conquers that fear.

—NELSON MANDELA

The elements to courage are simple: Take risks, especially on yourself, be uncomfortable, never assume, and explore without limitations.

- Take calculated risks. You will not only train your brain to respond better in unknown situations, but constantly level up your environment.
- Be uncomfortable. Speak publicly, travel, learn new languages, push yourself. Only when you decide in your mind that you are ready will you truly become comfortable with the discomfort of growth.
- Live by your own expectations, not those of others.
- Don't assume anything except there are always people smarter, braver, and more beautiful than you. You are only competing against yourself, and you should accept others as they are. Communicate.
- Explore the world around you. Find new perspectives to old situations.

PART 3

AUTHENTICITY

Authenticity (noun): the quality of being true to one's own personality, spirit, or character

AUTHENTICITY

Authenticity starts in the heart.

—BRIAN D'ANGELO

Total authenticity from within is one of the most difficult aspects of having conversations because you need to separate yourself from the current moment and determine if what is happening is in line with who you are. It's about honesty with yourself.

I have always considered myself to be a ruthlessly honest person, but a conversation with Amanda Gore set my mind off in a whirlwind. Amanda Gore is a physiotherapist with a major in psychology and a master practitioner of neurolinguistics. She is also a professional speaker and motivator with expertise in leadership, communication, relationships, lifestyle, and stress. I reached out to Gore in hopes of interviewing her, and she was more than happy to connect with me and answer my questions.

I was ready. My questions were prepared, and my research on Amanda Gore's life and work in front of me. As always, we started our Zoom call off with a bit of small talk. She asked me where I was from, told me how impressive it is

I am writing a book at such an early age, and questioned why I am exploring this topic as an engineering major. Gore pushed back at every explanation I gave.

"It's a great safety net. If I fail at whatever it is I am involved in, I can work as an engineer," I answered her question, my response prepared because this was a common question I received.

"But what are you passionate about?" she asked.

Silence.

"Seems to me all your reasons for doing it are interesting. They're very practical. They're very sensible. But it doesn't seem to have much to do with passion."

Silence.

"Well, if you could be anything you want to be, what would you be?"

"A dolphin trainer."

"A dolphin trainer. Why don't you go do that?"

"I don't think it would work. My family has put so much time and energy into my education, and this is not the type of life they see for me."

"Therein lies your problem. Rather than interviewing me, it's probably better for you to stop and think about the stories you've been told and you're telling yourself. It sounds to me, although I've not spent any time with you, you're fulfilling your others' desires and not yours. As a consequence, the lack of satisfaction or fulfillment is driving you into all sorts of other things you may or may not have chosen to go into," she paused. "So why are *you* doing engineering?" she asked again.

"I don't know. It teaches you how to think, it prepares you for any possible job and role. These are skills you can use everywhere. I don't know what else I would be doing!" I said, thinking out loud.

"You'd be training dolphins," was the frank response I received, and did not want to hear. "Because obviously engineering is not really what you want to do, or you're doing it because you truly, truly, truly believe it's a fabulous idea to have a profession you can fall back on. It would be really good to choose one you actually have a vague interest in or would be happy doing. What might that be?"

I described my recent interest in psychology, specifically in terms of the research I was doing with the book, and the topics that had piqued my curiosity in recent months.

"You look a little more alive when you talk about that."

"Yes, well I think that most things excite me more than engineering."

"Oh, so you would rather do anything else than engineering? You will make one lousy engineer, then, and you'll certainly never actually go through with finding and retaining an engineering job. You'll be miserable," she responded, and we continued with the rest of our conversation.

There is something to be said about getting a career in something you can do, but you absolutely hate. Surprise: You're never going to do it.

I was not prepared for this. I figured I would have a quick twenty-minute conversation about her life, and then have the opportunity to dissect the things she said. Rather, she had turned the tables and broke down my last few months of work into something very simple: fear.

Are you guided by fear? Do you stray from fear? Do you know what you are truly afraid of? I am, I do, and I think so. That is why authenticity is something I have adopted as a personal value, taking more time to finish my degree in classes I enjoyed, surrounded by supportive individuals.

It is with this in mind that you should build your life and your career around. You can do so by breaking everything down into three steps: having transparency in your thinking, realistic action, and evaluating the resulting synergy (or lack thereof).

PURPOSEFUL THINKING IN AVOIDING GOAL-RELIANCE

The bigger the picture, the more unique the potential human contribution. Our greatest strength is the exact opposite of narrow specialization. It is the ability to integrate broadly.

—DAVID EPSTEIN

Imagine life as a map. You are in an unknown jungle with no access to Wi-Fi or a cellular network. You're stranded and all you know is you want to survive and make it out of the jungle, and you only know two points on the map: where you are and where the exit is. You start walking directly forward, your nose in the paper, eyes on the ground. You are determined to make it home for tomorrow's dinner. You keep walking and walking. Then, you set up camp for the night, wake up at sunrise, and make it back for dinner. You have accomplished your goal, and you are content. You are safely home.

Comparably, if you live with blinders on in life, you will probably achieve your goal. You will be safe, home, and *okay*, but will this be the *best*-case scenario? What if the unknown is actually what you didn't know you needed?

Now, you are in the same jungle, holding the map in your hand with a general understanding of the way out, and an expectation you will be back in civilization in the next few days. As you're wandering in the greenery, you look around in awe. Suddenly, a beautiful waterfall, glistening in the sunlight, catches your eye. It would be out of the way to go to the waterfall, as it is not straight on your path toward the exit. It does not fit into your immediate goal of exiting the jungle as fast, and as safely, as possible.

Still, you turn off the path, noting on the map where you turned. You jump into the water, only to find this is the softest and warmest natural body of water you've ever been in. Your skin instantly feels softer and, as a whole, you are refreshed. On your way back, you notice some of the world's rarest and most beautiful flowers. By nightfall, you return to the original path, settle in for the night, and return home the following day.

Both scenarios get you home, but they serve to emphasize the idea the most direct route, provided by goal-reliance, is not necessarily the best (or most fulfilling, exciting, etc.) one. This does not mean to go outside and throw out your to-do list. Setting goals is not bad, nor is it a negative influence. It is the inability to deconstruct long-term goals into smaller ones, and use goals as a source of guidance, rather than a strict rulebook, that makes goal-reliance detrimental (Garvin and Margolis, 2015).

First, figure out what is important to you. Then, use goals to guide you there. Not the other way around.

In the most classic of Disney stories, *Cinderella*, the lovely orphan girl has one simple goal: leaving her current life of servitude to her stepmother and marrying the beautiful prince. The viewer goes on the journey with Cinderella and watches her relationship with the Fairy Godmother unfold, but we all know the expected ending of marriage to the prince. If you think about the Disney fairytale ending mentality in the context of your life, there are likely goals you have meant to achieve for many years. What will you do after?

I grew up in a Russian Jewish household where family means everything. We are a very tight-knit group of people who interact day to day. I could talk to my grandmother, who lives across the world, in the morning (her night), and a few hours later, I will talk to my sister about the same topic. Surprise! She already knows. She heard from my mom, who heard from her aunt, who heard it from my grandma. This community we have built up all over the globe, as the younger generations scattered, instilled certain expectations for me from a young age. You can probably guess Mom's favorite question to ask me on the phone: "Have you found yourself a nice boyfriend yet?" Of course, I have other goals in my life, including a career and personal growth, but this is a question that comes up frequently. It is a goal to find an eligible husband, have kids, and create the same level of familial bond my mom raised me with.

So does Cinderella. Cinderella has the goal of getting out of her present situation at the foreground, with the solution to all of her problems being the prince, but we, as readers and viewers, never get to see what happens after she rides off into the sunset as a newlywed in her glorious carriage.

That is why my recent thought process in regard to goals have been, "What then?" It is most definitely important to me to find a life partner, but that will not *solve* my problems. If I do not know how to interact with them, there is no talking about a relationship. If I cannot provide for myself and my family, then there is no talking about children. Once I *can* do these things, should I? Am I at the point when I have the maturity to teach a little human to live by my example?

It is all a process. Goal-reliance creates a mentality of focus on specifics, but we must actually shift our focus. By focusing on the background, we act with our values in mind, and become more transparent with ourselves when thinking. The thoughts become, "Is this the right time?" or, "Am I acting in accordance with what is important to me?" This will stop you from ending up having accomplished your goal but losing yourself in the process.

Whenever you think of some goal, or endpoint, think about what your life will look like after. What happens next?

Goals are usually things we *want* but *have difficulty achieving* even when we know they are achievable. Otherwise, we wouldn't need a goal in the first place.

The athletic world sees the repercussions of goal-reliance all the time. When newcomers make their way to the gym, with a hefty goal of losing forty pounds or gaining 15 percent muscle mass in the next month, trainers maintain everything is about maintaining a healthy and fit lifestyle, and simply achieving these immediate body goals will only hurt you (Choi, 2020).

Two summers ago, my mom and I signed up for a six-week fitness challenge. We had to pay $700 to the gym, but if we either lost twenty pounds or 5 percent body fat by the end of the challenge, the money would be returned to us.

We went to the gym each and every day. The first few days were killers; bending down was impossible. Because of the strict nutrition plan we were provided, the first two or three weeks were full of sugar-withdrawal, and I was angry and unapproachable. Nevertheless, my mom and I got through the challenge, ate healthy, lost the weight, gained muscle, and rejoiced upon receiving our money back at the end. Our goal was achieved!

Not. Three months later, both of us were back to where we were prior to the challenge, not going to the gym, and eating sugar (oops). Long term, this was something that made us feel great, strong, and proud of ourselves. We had achieved such a great feat, and there was a big fat checkmark next to "Six-Week Fitness Challenge," but it did not hold. If we had abandoned the specific goal of losing a certain amount of weight and made a general goal of being more fit and healthy, we would likely still use the gym membership, instead of solely being charged for one.

Since then, I picked up boxing and lifting weights. Without a certain weight in mind on a specific timeline, I have been able to enjoy it, learn, and grow with each workout. Slowly, I began to feel a difference in my mood, and now the gym is a part of my daily routine, not because I am forced to go or need to, but because I want to.

> *Avoiding focusing on short-term, fleeting goals will prevent you falling into the trap of instant gratification and give you an edge over those around you; you'll see whether things are actually important, and if so, why.*

This idea of avoiding goal-reliance and allowing yourself to see the big picture shows up with Phyllis Lantos, the former CFO of New York Presbyterian Hospital. This is a brilliant woman who graduated from MIT with a degree in mathematics but an interest in healthcare. She wrote her thesis on planning mental health systems, so when she was assigned a job in addiction services working for the City of New York, she quickly became the liaison between the operations and budget office. Lantos embarked on learning all the terminology required for both the medical and financial aspects of the role, which was then expanded to oversee a budget of over a billion dollars.

This began her life-long career in healthcare avoiding goal-reliance. Instead of focusing on the next prospective role that would represent the next rung on the corporate ladder, Phyllis followed the opportunities presented, applying herself fully to learn and excel in each position.

Lantos still remembers her transition to the Montefiore Hospital, noting the dynamic in the office at the very beginning of her twenty-year career there: each person had a specific role, whether it be reimbursement or budget. It didn't matter what their job was though because one commonality existed between all of the men working there, namely that they spoke "finance."

In this scenario, many individuals would have said "I'm out" and called it a day. Lantos did not have experience in finance, and she didn't know the terminology the men around her were using. She dove into the detailed theories that would explain how the concepts were established, using their skills to translate the finance language to non-finance staff.

Phyllis focused on the impact each group might have on any given other. If the operations group wanted to increase resources, Phyllis would work through budgets to determine how to reduce hospital expenses, and the skills she needed for the job came along the way. She soon found her role in the team as a translator, switching between finance, IT, and operations. She understood the numbers and supported the non-finance staff to optimize their performance.

Very quickly, this became her value. When she had to move for her husband's fellowship, she was handed a forty-pound portable computer unit, which required setting up its own network in whatever location she would be. Lantos' priorities falling outside of goal-reliance allowed her to contribute to the team and self-actualize in her role.

> *The ability to zoom out and have a bird's eye view will set you apart because it isn't a natural thought process. We tend to get bogged down in the details, leading to goal-reliance.*

Similarly, here is a story about a woman named Mary Sue.[1] Mary was a psychology undergrad through post-doc and was able to have a successful career in engineering because of her resiliency in the field and ability to zoom out. After she finished her post-doctoral fellowship, the job prospects were limited, and she did what she had to do: took a job that was not interesting to her at a local university, where she worked for one year.

As I heard Mary's story, Amanda Gore's words were at the back of my head: a person with no interest in their job will not stay there for long.

While Mary was working at the university, she attended a psychology conference to present her dissertation, where she met a nationally recognized electrical engineer who promised to sponsor Mary. That is how Mary, a psychologist, ended up working in business and technology, among all engineers.

Just as the students felt out of place when they were told they would have to write a book by Eric, Mary wasn't in her optimal environment among these incredibly technically trained engineers. She didn't understand the

---

1   The names and identifying details of this story have been anonymized, and the story has been adjusted to fit the content of this book.

language they were using, or the requests her boss was making. She told me how she circumvented this issue and was able to find her place in the company.

She walked around with an empty journal and created a dictionary of all the words she didn't know. She wrote them down when they were mentioned in passing, and then would find the least threatening person around to ask what they meant. By the end of the year, she worked with the engineers and the executive directors and increased the company profit by nearly 500 percent. The results spoke for themselves more than any degree in engineering could have.

In both of these situations, the individuals were able to recognize their role in the organization, educational preparation, and background in the field, and understand if they sit there and try to understand all of the details, they will never succeed on the job. There are specialists who work on one particular project, such as the mechanical engineers who produce the cap or the bottle of a perfume, the chemists who create the liquid, and the marketing team who presents you with the advertising. They took one step back and realized a key point: having a complete landscape allows you to see the whole field.

You are the project manager of your life, and if you do not zoom out enough to have a full view, you will lose focus of what it important.

The ability to zoom out and take a managerial role in your own life is something companies tend to encourage. The reasoning behind this: a company structure that does not limit employees to their current skills is one that allows them to pursue personal interests, thus improving output and performance (Velasco, Batista-Foguet and Emmerling, 2019). For instance, at Proctor and Gamble, a leading company in the consumer goods industry, employees are given the opportunity to work on numerous projects simultaneously and then change locations or "brands" every few years, simulating working in an entirely new company (Committee on Department of Homeland Security Occupational Health and Operational Medicine Infrastructure, 2014). This not only prevents goal-reliance, but enforces a culture of creativity, progress, and authenticity in goal-setting.

The prevalence of goal-reliance certainly seeps its way into the professional world, especially because of the financial and social difficulties that may come with following your heart. In one of my interviews, the person I spoke to is a religious leader, and he expressed his opinions about certain professions in colorful language. "They're forced to do awful things, and the engineers hate it because it's dull as dishwater." He went on to express that these generalizations do not apply to everyone, but specifically the people who chose the wrong profession as a result of not following their hearts. He explained engineers come to his religious organization and find themselves exceptionally happy doing volunteer work, losing themselves in developing programs that are solely for the purpose of civil engagement. Others cannot bear the pressures that come with their professional role and turn to religion as an escape.

Sometimes, avoiding goal-reliance means following your heart. This can be the most difficult step, and it is something I struggle with day-to-day.

For instance, at Vanderbilt, given the restrictive schedule an engineering degree provides, most advisors are apprehensive when students take on multiple majors that will prevent true exploration of interests. My advisor looked at me like I was absolutely insane when I proposed picking up a math double major and three minors.

"Why don't you see how you like those classes first? Try a higher-level math class, then decide if you want the major," he asked me, making it more of a suggestion than a question.

"No, I know for sure this is the right path, and I'm going to go through with it," I replied confidently, in typical Ester fashion. About three months later, I withdrew from the math class I was enrolled in, dropped the math major, and went along my merry way to my advisor to tell him that he was right.

For non-engineers, Vanderbilt takes a completely different path. The students cannot declare a major until their sophomore year, and they are not given a specific advisor until they do find the major they are interested in. For many, the advice given by their advisor is simple: Take the classes you're interested in and you'll see a pattern will emerge. Worst case, you'll have to take an extra class or two for the major requirements. Those few extra classes are the materialization step we are talking about it in this section.

Involve yourself in activities in line with who you are, instead of setting goals and matching activities to those goals.

A few months ago, I spoke to my brother about goals. He is thirteen but quite observant. I was discussing my book and how the winter break will give me a wonderful opportunity to write and organize my thoughts on life. He looked at me and smiled. Then he said something along the lines of, "So last winter break, you found yourself a boyfriend to fill your time, and now it's the book? What will you do next winter break?"

A simple statement. A true one, too, but it points to my own goal-reliance. We live in a society where goals are overabundant, but discerning for yourself which ones are yours, which will excite and invigorate you, is crucial.

In writing this book, I had to reevaluate the *why* behind the goal for publishing something. Yes, it would look great on a resume and is something to brag about. It's also an exorbitant amount of work, and Eric Koester, the person who runs the program, explained that to me before he popped the million-dollar question: What is your goal in writing a book? I came up with a quick answer about helping people, sharing the knowledge I had acquired from those around me, and some other things that came to mind. Eric pushed further: What is the goal in writing this book?

Although I didn't have an answer that satisfied him at the time, it remained at the back of my mind, and I really struggled with defining the structure and content of the book for the first few months because I didn't have the goal presented for me. I knew the timeline of publication, but I did not know *why*. Now I've realized I write with the goal of organizing my thoughts, understanding myself and fulfillment better, and learning from wise and accomplished individuals. It is about my personal growth and sharing that with others is just the cherry on top.

> *Knowing your why makes setting healthy goals much easier. Your goals should be personal to make them really count.*

The idea of personal growth through goal-setting is nothing new. It is a way to challenge yourself by quantifying where you want to see yourself in a certain amount of time. It is important to keep these to yourself, though, and create alignment between intention and action, and it needs to be *personal*.

Surprisingly, it was found people who announce their goals are less likely to accomplish them. In 1982, Peter Gollwitzer wrote a book on substitution, the act of doing a lesser task instead of a bigger one (e.g., talking instead of doing), and then conducted a study in 2009. One hundred and sixty-three people across four separate tests wrote down their goals, half of which announced their intention to work on this task. Forty-five minutes were allotted to work on the task that would allow them to accomplish the goal, and the group that did not share their intentions far outperformed the "talkers." Weird, right? It all starts from the motivation. If something is authentic, and important to you, then it is personal (Sivers, 2010). Through purposeful thinking, it is possible to create a relationship with yourself, keeping you accountable to the challenges you set and then acting on them in a healthy manner. It appears you just need to go for it and truly listen to your gut.

Vicki Heyman, author of *The Art of Diplomacy*, co-founder of Uncharted, LLC, philanthropist at heart, and Vanderbilt Owen School of Management graduate, shared her story of meeting and developing a relationship with her husband. At first, they were acquaintances. She was an art history and business major; he was an economics major. She was involved in Greek life, and he was involved on campus. They knew each other but were not close friends. They shared some of the same undergraduate classes, and Vicki was a little sister in Bruce's fraternity, but they had never dated and weren't in the same group of friends. However, when Vicki applied for, and was accepted by, the accelerated program with the Owen Graduate School of Management, there was only one other student she knew who was in a similar situation: her future husband, Bruce Heyman.

At this point, she decided to advance their level of relationship from "we maybe know each other, the other person looks kind of cool" to "let's be peers!" She proposed the idea of working with him on a group project for one of the possible classes they could take. "With your brains and my creativity, we can get an A," Vicki said. Not soon after, Bruce asked Vicki to go on a date, and she knew this meant studying would be over. They developed a yin-yang style relationship and would rarely be found apart, so when it came time to graduate, Bruce proposed.

Let's pause for a moment here and note this was about forty years ago, and a long-distance relationship was simply impossible. It was time to jump in or walk their separate ways, and the setting, which provided high external pressures, wasn't helping. There is the perfect example of how goal-reliance can stand in the way of a truly authentic and purposeful lifestyle. Vicki had her goals, and Bruce had his. They chose to follow their hearts on this one, and are now living together happily, having recently celebrated their forty-first year of marriage.

The notion of following your heart as it relates to goals is not one that pertains solely to love or romantic interests. Goal setting actually helps with a sense of purpose, especially when done to a healthy degree (Schippers and Ziegler, 2019). Paul M. Kurtz, associate dean and J. Alton Hosch Professor Emeritus at the University of Georgia Law School, *loved* what he did and you can tell.

As a child (and to this very day), Kurtz loved to chat. He did well in school, made his parents proud, and there was a certain expectation from him to not only attain a bachelor's degree, but continue on to some form of graduate school. From a young age, he assumed this was law school, a steppingstone to his career as a lawyer. This was the goal he had in mind, and he dared to stray from it—a purposeful and authentic thought process that allowed him to self-actualize.

At the time Professor Kurtz was graduating from his undergraduate years at Vanderbilt, men were being drafted to serve in the Vietnam War. Because of this, his planned attendance at the University of Virginia Law School could have been interrupted and caused him to restart the material from the beginning. The timing wasn't right, and eventually the location did not work either. He waited a year to get drafted (which never happened) and came to realize he wanted to be near his current girlfriend, now his wife of fifty years. Vanderbilt Law School, not the University of Virginia, was the place for him.

Recognize what's not you and move on. No need to stick to a plan that doesn't work anymore.

He spent the summer after his first year working for a law firm composed of two men, in his hometown of about six thousand people, where his dad was mayor. This summer was pivotal for Kurtz's career because he began to understand working at a small firm would mean representing people when they bought houses, or helping teenagers in traffic, or working on wills. Even though these were important things, he questioned whether this was for him. During his second year, he came to realize a future in a large law firm was not likely in the cards after interviewing for law firms for a second-summer clerkship was unavailing. A year and a half into law school, Professor

Kurtz had a daunting realization: He did not want to be a lawyer. This was not the lifestyle he wanted.

"I felt like the risk of that was that after twenty, thirty, or forty years, I'd wake up one morning and say, 'What have you done with your life, you know, you're president of the Kiwanis Club, you bowl regularly, play golf, have a nice living?'" He points out he knew his life would have been fine, but he did not feel true to himself. He didn't believe he was challenging himself to his fullest ability, and he wanted to find something that would cater to his needs on an intellectual level but also match his personality in a way he understood law practice would never be able to. It started by analyzing what he genuinely liked doing and what he was good at: He was good at and enjoyed law school. Kurtz had not strayed from the challenge law school presents, but rather welcomed it and enjoyed every second of it. He was a reader and writer at heart, and the foundations of our legal system are what got Kurtz excited. That was when he came to the realization being a law professor would be something he would enjoy and be good at.

From there, the road was clear: LLM at Harvard, which was the standard for any aspiring law professors, a year break while he searched for a job and his wife taught at a parochial elementary school, and then moving to Athens, Georgia, to begin his impeccable career as a professor at the University of Georgia School of Law.

"We came here on my three-year plan, and now we've been here and served forty-five years. They can't even fire me anymore because I quit!" (Actually, he retired in 2013.) While on the UGA faculty, he taught criminal law, family law, and constitutional law, he served as the associate dean for academic and student affairs for University of Georgia's Law School for twenty-two years and was named a J. Alton Hosch Professor of Law in 1994, a prestigious position, and he is now professor emeritus. He has written books and articles and done a lot of non-profit work and law reform. He loved the metrics of getting things done and measured his success by the final results.

This will be your key to understanding where your heart lies: Does the process excite you? Are you engaged? Are you happy?

If you looked at Kurtz's resume, it might seem like this was the plan. There was a mission from the very beginning to become a law professor, and everything is laid out perfectly to achieve that goal. But this is not true; there were curves and obstacles in between, among them the purposeful thinking required for him to become his best, and fullest, self.

I challenge you to think about the last action you took that was your decision, for the purpose of impacting you long term. Now think about how this action plays into your greater goals. If you have an overarching goal of becoming a rock enthusiast, then finding one geological interesting piece of sediment may be an achievement in itself.

Overall, goals should be about your state and lifestyle, rather than a specific point. If they allow for constant culminations, your life will be filled with rising actions. If they do not, you will peak early and be lost. You will have to reinvent your life, rediscover who you are, which is significantly more difficult.

THINK BIG AND IDENTIFY YOUR TRUE "WHY"

The best day of your life is the one on which you decide your life is your own. No apologies or excuses. No one to lean on, rely on, or blame. The gift is yours—it is an amazing journey—and you alone are responsible for the quality of it. This is the day your life really begins.

—BOB MOAWAD

If I were to look at your life's work and hobbies, would I know who you are? A team player, interested in cross-cultural impacts on organizations, an individual with family values? Or maybe a leader passionate about lasting environmental change? An athlete, but curious about the brain's function? All of these intersectional identities come together to define you on a higher level: Who are you? Why do you do the things you do?

From a biological perspective, there are three fundamental ways to process any situation: on the primal level, you would answer the question *how* (Thioux, Gazzola and Keysers, 2008). This is an observation, like noting I sit in front of the computer to type, quickly. Then, on an intermediate level, it is answering the question *what*, a more analysis-based thinking which connects the physical action to the larger picture. I am writing a chapter for the book. Finally, the *why* requires the highest level of processing: linking the analyzed action to other occurring events. My editor will be mad if I miss a deadline, so I need to work on a chapter. With each rising level, more neurons are at work because it is more difficult for the brain to connect the current action with the previous ones it has seen. That is why reaching the highest level of information processing, or really pondering the *why* is difficult, particularly so on a large scale. Similarly, you must approach your life with this three-level mentality but work backward.

Thinking big to identify your why will take the most mental energy, but once this is done, everything else falls into place.

There is no requirement for the number of actions you take (what), or the way in which you take them (how), as long as they serve your greater purpose (why). That is why, we will explore the life of an internationally recognized veterinarian and researcher who *hated school*. This is the story Boaz Arzi tells.

Boaz was a very bad student. He got kicked out of schools in Israel to the point where his middle school specialized in car mechanics, and even from there, he got kicked out. His parents signed him up for an external private school, but there were two problems. First, Boaz's seat was right near the window, and the window had a beautiful view of the sea. The second problem was Boaz is a surfer. This meant every time the wave would come up, Boaz would escape the classroom, and he would surf. When his teacher confronted him, explaining he knew what Boaz was doing, Boaz took a more creative route. He would keep his school bag in the bathroom, request to use the restroom, and then once again escape.

As a result, Boaz was not a good student. He also did not score well on the Israeli version of the SAT because he was not in school to take it. That is why when he moved to the US and took the SAT (which he discovered was being administered upon walking into school that morning), he received marks solely for writing down his name. School did not fulfill Boaz, and for him, surfing was more important than school, which was just not a good fit at the time.

Upon graduation, he served in the Israeli Defense Forces (IDF), after which he desperately needed a job. No one was hiring a student with truly terrible grades, atrocious SAT scores, and nothing more than a childhood dream to become a veterinarian. He did not know what he was doing, nor did he understand what was taught to him in school, but he got a job as a veterinary assistant at a veterinary clinic.

At this point, Boaz points out his life started to have a semblance of purpose.

When you find your purpose, it feels right. Things click.

"Okay, I need to start doing stuff with my life," he thought, and went over to the MIT-equivalent in Israel with the request to take the pre-requisite course for attendance. The secretary expressed, honestly, his scores were the lowest he had ever seen but allowed him to take the exam. Unsurprisingly, he failed the exam to be allowed to take the pre-pre-university courses.

The veterinarian Boaz was working for then asked him a question that has come up a few times in this book now: Why?

"Why are you going there? What do you want to do with your life?"

"I want to be an engineer," was met with a smile and a response Boaz did not expect.

"You? An engineer? No…you are a natural born veterinarian."

This was the inflection point for Boaz' career, from where he met with the University of Haifa's biology department chair, who listened to Boaz' story, and promised him if he passed the pre-pre-undergraduate course, he would admit him to the biology department. Boaz immediately enrolled and studied intensely. Right after taking and barely passing the final exam, his teacher told him, "You passed it, but nothing good is going to come out of you."

From there, all Boaz has done was prove the mathematics teacher wrong. He was admitted to the University of Haifa Biology Program and then to a top veterinary school in Budapest, Hungary, at which point he was getting straight As in all tests. Upon completion of veterinary school, he returned to work with the same vet who he had worked with so many years before, who had encouraged him to embark on this career. Today, Boaz is a full-time professor at the School of Veterinary Medicine at UC Davis and regarded as one of the top veterinary dentists and maxillofacial surgeons in the field, as well as a world leader in veterinary regenerative medicine. He is also known as the surfer-professor by his students and colleagues.

It is clear from Boaz' story how purpose, and a clear answer to *why,* guided him significantly. How will you allow it to guide you?

Using your why to guide you will lead you your fate: the result of the choices you make.

Remember, the more brain the work has to do up front, the more it will avoid it. Putting in the up-front energy expenditure hard tasks require is not something to look forward to, like trying difficult math problems for the very first time without peeking at the answer key. Finding purpose is even harder than math, believe it or not, which is why identifying your "why" is something that often gets lost in translation, especially for young students vying for a seat at a good university.

Looking back on the college admissions process, one of the most difficult questions for me to answer, especially for the Ivy League universities, was "Why us?" Thinking logically, there wasn't anything that really set one school apart from the other. All of them have incredible academics, high expectations for campus involvement, stellar financial aid packages, and unparalleled alumni networks. I desperately tried to delineate the differences between the schools, in terms of the *type* of people who generally attend each university: are they quirky, nerdy, adventurous? Instead of thinking about my own reasoning for applying (outside of the excellent education each of these institutions would offer), I was thinking about what they might expect from me. This was not the way to go about it, and definitely something I would discourage future applicants from doing.

This is probably why I was not ultimately accepted by many of these elite schools, despite being a large part of my school and hometown community, maintaining excellent grades, and devoting my free hours to research in a lab. My *why* was not clear to me, and it most definitely was not coming across clearly to the admissions officer reading my file. To them, I was just another student trying to gain admission to a top school and would say whatever necessary to do so, and I was.

Instead of thinking about what made me unique, I was trying to fit a mold. The problem with this thinking is we all hold a truly distinctive combination of skills, talents, and personality that makes it virtually impossible for anyone else to be exactly the same. Judaic belief states each soul is brought to earth because it is needed. As such, anything in existence is only here because a higher power decided this should be here in this very moment. We were not all meant to be doctors because then no one would need to be healed. We were not all meant to be painters because then no one would cook, or clean, or educate. Each of us has our own individual mission and purpose, and something clicks once we find it. Many people call this "passion."

Your why, and the work you do around it, is what separates you from those around you and makes you unique.

In early January, I received a message from a random woman who had found my name on Facebook and wanted me to speak with her daughter, a Vanderbilt Class of 2026 applicant. I agreed to speak with the girl, who we'll refer to as Amanda, and started the conversation by asking what activities she was involved in. She rattled off the traditional and expected roles: president of x club, social media chair of y club, volunteer at the local hospital, camp counselor, etc. I sat there and listened, and then followed with another question, which is exactly what this chapter is about: What are you passionate about? The girl took a moment, and then began to tell me about her passion for being a part of the community. Hearing her response took me back to what my response would have been three years ago: I enjoy helping people, and that's why I'm involved in x, y, and z.

"Amanda, I'm not asking you for the scripted response you would give to an admissions officer," I explained to her, drawing parallels from my own experience and thinking about what I wished someone had told me. "I'm asking you *why* you are involved in all of these organizations, which seem like they have nothing to do with each other."

She paused again. I could feel I was potentially causing her anxiety, so I used my involvement at Vanderbilt as an example. "Amanda, I am a member of the Executive Board of the Multicultural Leadership Council at Vanderbilt because I think it's important we recognize and celebrate the cultural diversity we have on campus and then take tangible steps to bringing people of different backgrounds together. That's also why I'm a part of the campus Hillel, Chabad, and even Dore for a Day. In each of these organizations, I get to interact with people one-on-one and have interesting discussions with an individual who wants to learn and is willing to change. I gain a lot of perspective from them, too."

"I think for me, it is really important the community members I interact with have good mental health," Amanda mustered up, talking slowly, seemingly unsure of herself. "I don't like to see people in pain. When I volunteer with the American Cancer Association, I work with the patients and build impactful relationships. I like to see them happy. It's the same with the kids at camp; I get to be a guiding force in their upbringing, especially if they come back every year. I see them grow and progress, and I help them through any mental issues they may be going through. With them, and some of the other organizations I'm a part of, I got to raise money for the American Cancer Association."

As Amanda kept talking, she gained confidence. She had identified her why.

"Amanda, from here, it's up to you. Continue exploring that passion and allow the causes that are important to you to guide you, not what looks good on paper," I told her, feeling really proud of myself for helping her avoid this pitfall.

Find the commonalities between actions you enjoy. They'll lead you to your why.

This is a similar point many admissions officers in elite private universities make. A Duke University admissions officer, Rachel Toor, explains when they are reading the files or interviewing the students, they are looking to fall in love with the individual: how they express themselves, how they view their world, what they expect their impact to be, and how they have already started and expect to continue achieving it (John, 2016). Their application should speak for itself; their life work should give the admissions committee a glimpse of who they are and what their life looks like. Their values should shine through.

"As an admissions officer, you're picking people to enroll in your community, your space, for the next four years. They're going to choose who they like and who they want to get to know," Toor says (John, 2016). She continues by explaining it doesn't matter what the specific activity or passion is, as long as the student is doing *something interesting*. "Founding a club or starting a program in your community shows initiative. Teaching yourself to play guitar is viable, and it's something people don't think about."

This is once again a display of the purpose we are searching for and a description of the *why*. I know firsthand a high-stress environment, like a competitive high school entirely geared for college admissions, can influence you in the direction of doing the *what* and the *how*, and making up a *why*.

Think "why," then work around that.

In the larger scope of life, these little things, like volunteering for a specific organization or planning events for another, all add up. Looking back on my high school years, I wish I was more purposeful in where I devoted my time instead of creating fictional "why's" in my head. I would not have been in the Yearbook Club, School Newspaper, Jewish Club, Science Competition Club, Math and Chess Club, and the school musical. Now, I recognize just how important it is to really think big to identify your why. I would have chosen what I felt most passionate about—directing the musical—and devoted the majority of my time to it.

That is the advice an MIT graduate and current alumni admissions interviewer said when she was telling me about a recent file that had landed in her stack. This was an extraordinary student who presented himself professionally and respectfully, but he was not nearly as involved in school activities, or in his community, as the other applicants. One thing made him stand out, though.

"There was this one guy who does origami, which was like bizarro! I think chess, too, and he's just a master at both, working on them at a really extraordinary level in high school. He described to me how he was forty points short of making it to the next classification of chess player, but he was just determined to continue working at it, so he had traveled across the world for it. I thought to myself—he doesn't do any sports and isn't involved in music. Doesn't do this, he doesn't do that. I thought about it and realized, he's passionate, and he's really into it," she told me about this applicant.

The interviewer then described how the student showed her an example of a piece of origami with a napkin, and she points out it was some, "heavy duty origami, when in terms of angles and folding, and all this stuff it's very mathematical." The origami master was then admitted to MIT because he had expressed his passion and followed it throughout his high school career.

The ties between passion and purpose are almost inseparable. Because of the way our lives are structured, it is easy to get distracted from your true "why," and it is hard to define your purpose. Rather, there is increased pressure to live the perfect life, one motivated by more materialistic values than deeply rooted ones that go hand-in-hand with passion.

Research has shown goals a person sets themselves will enhance your wellbeing and further your self-determination. A step toward self-determination is a step toward a fulfilled, self-actualized lifestyle (Schippers and Ziegler, 2019). These goals are called self-concordant goals, ones that fulfill needs that are aligned with a person's values and passion, and there is a direct relationship between setting these and having improved wellbeing, higher vitality, a more meaningful life, and lowered depression.

Setting goals that align themselves with your "why" have psychological and physical health benefits.

Setting concordant and self-endorsed goals is something Abby McDonald Schwartz and Rashmi K. Drummond, the founders of Phi Sigma Rho, a national engineering sorority, are well aware of. As they told their story, their purpose of creating a welcoming space for women in engineering became apparent. Looking back, both pointed out the thing they are most proud of is not the external recognition for the founding of the organization, but rather having the courage and the devotion to creating an accessible community.

McDonald Schwartz and Drummond were freshmen engineering student at Purdue University, going through the rigorous coursework most engineering curriculums present: general chemistry, physics, and mathematics. Because of the difficulties that came with this material, they were constantly studying, making the balance between schoolwork and social time a complicated relationship.

Then, Abby decided to go through the sorority rush process, a generally time-consuming and emotionally exhausting pursuit of friendship, community, and sisterhood. As she learned more about the commitments that came with being in a sorority, she became overwhelmed. It would be virtually impossible to truly join the sisterhood and devote herself fully to the experience without losing focus in her engineering coursework.

So, Abby went and found out information on how to start an organization and found out the procedures to do so. She knocked on Rashmi's door, presenting the steps of action.

At this point, they had to make a decision. Was it worth it? Was this something the girls wanted to pursue at the very beginning of their college career, to devote their time and energy to? Did it match their values and speak to them on a personal level? Was there a *why*?

The answer to all of these was a resounding *yes*. This marked the beginning of a sorority for women in engineering, a place where young women could connect over their coursework and be encouraged in stressful times, a community that uplifted each individual, and a low-commitment sisterhood based on mutual understanding.

"There's two things that really define the way we live our lives," Rashmi explained. "One is what choices we make when we're faced with a decision. How do we respond to what life throws at us? When Abby came by and brought this up, it would have been easy to say that this would be too much work and would take up too much time…and the second thing is who we surround ourselves with. You need to find people who will support you and talk you up. Whenever I had doubts about anything, Abby would build me up, and I would do the same for her. We were fortunate enough to have found each other, and the stars aligned so we were able to support each other through the process of founding the sorority."

Not only did McDonald Schwartz and Drummond find a purpose in their sorority, but they had also found key members of their respective A-Teams. What more could they ask for?

Looking back, the founders point out nothing you do is ever in a vacuum. Their "why" was to create a ripple of change and make sure women in engineering had a space to connect. They saw the fruits of their labors at the twenty-fifth anniversary of Phi Sigma Rho, where a hotel ballroom was full of amazingly smart women in all shapes, sizes, colors, and backgrounds.

"It makes us so excited to hear people's stories about how much Phi Sigma Rho has helped them get through engineering, pushed them to learn, and improved their personal lives," McDonald said after I shared that never in my life would I have imagined myself as an individual joining a sorority. It did not seem like the path for me, but when I learned about the existence of Phi Sigma Rho at Vanderbilt, it seemed to click.

Despite the difficulties associated with starting an organization on your own, especially in a new setting, McDonald Schwartz and Drummond were able to succeed. This is because of the fulfillment of the basic psychological needs to autonomy and competence setting such goals brings about (Ryan and Deci, 2001). Instead of chasing "happiness," or letting the outside world define the life the women should live in college, they chose to create their own college experience according to their preferences, helping prevent burn-out, depression, and a lack of experienced meaning—common issues people who follow others' purpose will have (Suh, Gnilka and Rice, 2017).

Sometimes this can be as simple as mindset. A recent LinkedIn post by Eric Koester, the founder of the Creative Writer's Institute, shared a specific interaction he had with one of his students. This student was confused about her future career path post-graduation, and she wanted Eric's help. Eric asked her, "What do you want to do every day?" to which she answered, "I have been looking at jobs in finance, data science, and..."

Here, Eric makes an important distinction: "Find out what someone does every day at their job, not just the title." He pushed his student to learn the activities that take place every day on each of the roles she was looking for and directed her to YouTube, Google, and Facebook in search of informational interviews. He made something very clear: You are not just taking on the marketed terms that are used in the job title, or the six-figure salary; you are accepting the responsibilities and all of the possible consequences (both positive and negative) that come with the job.

> *Dig beyond the level of "what" or "how." Why do you want to do something? Do the expectations that come with doing this work for you? What will you actually be doing? How does this fit into your larger purpose?*

This key understanding of responsibility and expectations is something Gabriella Marvaldi, daughter of two Olympian skaters, understands all too well. Being brought into the world by parents Isabelle Brasseur and Rocky Marval (Marvaldi), the dynamic in her home growing up was strange, to say the least. Something she pointed out in an interview was her original push to start skating at four years old. Her parents did not want their daughter to be a skater because they were aware of the expectations that came with it. Gabriella's grandmother said, "No, she's going to be a skater."

The next sixteen years of the young woman's life turned into constant training: waking up at 7:00 a.m., being at the rink by 8:30 a.m., warming up until 9:00 a.m., and skating for the next five hours. This became a full-time job, making high school an online experience and changing Gabriella's perspective on life. Long term, her heart was not in it, even though she loved the sport. She could not remain committed, and when quarantine started, Gabriella decided to move on to a new adventure: art school and majoring in social media management. She believes this is different because it's a new type of commitment, and one she is ready to make. She plans to devote her life to environmental protection through the digital imprint.

> *Understand the expectations that come with certain "whats," such as jobs or career shifts. Question their alignment with your "why."*

Nevertheless, sometimes it takes getting everything you were looking for to understand your new life simply does not fit your original expectations. In the case of Ryan Nicodemus, now known as one of *The Minimalists*, this was exactly so. Growing up poor was tough. There was white money (food stamps) and green money (real money) for Ryan, cockroaches in the kitchen, and on-and-off electricity. His mother had lost sight of the purpose, and the meaning of life, and Ryan felt the only way for him to never lose sight was to make a lot of money.

Ryan set a goal for himself: he would need to make a certain amount of money per year so he would never have to live in the same conditions he grew up in. He spent days and nights working just for the sake of changing his living conditions without ever really thinking about whether he enjoyed what he did. By twenty-eight years old, Ryan had achieved all of these goals: he was the youngest director in the company's over one hundred-year history, he had all of the benefits of such a job (including luxury cars, designer clothes, and a suburban house "with more toilets than people"), and he was living the American Dream.

It wasn't until his mother died he began to reassess this goal America had put out for him and the expectations came with it. There was an expectation to work endlessly with no end in sight. There was an expectation to worship *things* instead of *experiences*. Most importantly, this was the American Dream, and not Ryan's Dream. He had been accumulating debt for a lifestyle he didn't enjoy, and it took his mother's passing for him to realize he should quit his job and start thinking about the expectations for his life that he was okay with.

In the example of the now-minimalist, it took getting everything he thought he wanted to realize that wasn't what he wanted at all. There were unexpected consequences of his unclear understanding of what he wanted out of life. It wasn't his purpose to become a middle manager in the corporate world, nor was it to commit to working for a firm he felt did not care about him. His *why* had been getting out of poverty, but he should have thought about the influences that acted on them throughout his rise up the ladder.

The thing about minimalism is it forces you to be *purposeful*. You need to think about why you need certain items in your space and what they are contributing to your life (Becoming Minimalist). You aren't just cruising—it is intentional and brings much clarity as a result. Because of this clarity, there is improved focus on the important aspects of life.

Be purposeful with who, and what, you let into your space.

The notion something dramatic must happen for us to "open our eyes" is not uncommon, but sometimes our calling is actually right in front of us. It comes up in the story of current associate professor at Vanderbilt and executive coach Leonora Zilkha Williamson, a Princeton graduate and Harvard MBA recipient. After graduating with her top tier undergraduate and graduate degrees, she found her way to Wall Street, working at JPMorgan, the Boston Consulting Group (BCG), and then finding her way to Estee Lauder as an executive director of MAC's international marketing department.

Williamson believes coaching is one of those professions you are born with, and you are wired to do it from the moment you are old enough to understand it. The first job Williamson was ever paid for was helping a six-year-old girl who lived near her with spelling words and practicing her violin. At the age of eight, she already loved it, and soon began to actively seek out those kinds of opportunities. She was open to being coached herself, seeking out mentors in the people senior to her in the workplace, and early on in her career she began to mentor others.

What she found interesting about her job at JPMorgan was teaching, communicating, and sharing came naturally to her. She once gave a presentation to her peers on how to write a good PowerPoint deck. Throughout her career in corporate America, Williamson would sit through many corporate trainings, and each time she watched the trainer very carefully. She found herself jealous of their role in the organization because it looked like they had the most fun jobs. However, it never occurred to her this was a job she could do because she thought she was supposed to want some job with a "C" in the front of the title.

She points out her influence, like the minimalists, was corporate America. Upon making the decision to shift from working on Wall Street to coaching, she knew coaching isn't usually as lucrative as corporate jobs. There had been unconscious influences of wanting to earn money, but Williamson points out this simply was not her ultimate goal. That is why she made the decision to do coach training and open up a coaching practice, rather than find another corporate job. She believes coaching has the greatest alignment with who she is and what she cares about. Her story is one where heart truly took over mind.

What you want is often difficult to decipher. That's your why. What you want to want is influenced by your upbringing, culture, and environment. They are not always the same.

This is exactly what we are exploring: There is what you *want*, and there is what you *want to want*. For Leonora Zilkha Williamson, the former was the responsibility and expectations that come with being a trainer, and the latter was becoming a part of the C-suite on Wall Street with a corner office. She had been told her entire life this was the description of the perfect life, but subconsciously she only *wanted* to want this lifestyle. The moment Williamson realized this wasn't for her and she didn't care for this, she talks about a truly liberating feeling: She was at a point in her life to do what she loves to do and care about the things she wants to care about.

This marked the beginning of her coaching career: going to coaching school learning how to do it and committing herself fully. She understood the expectations and consequences: There would be a different pay, different cultural environment, different types of clients, etc. She made an intention to follow this path, and things started to fall into place for her. The opportunity to teach at Vanderbilt opened up, which Williamson remarks is wonderful because of her interactions with Gen Z and the joy teaching brings her.

Being able to really differentiate between her heart and what her mind had convinced her was the right path allowed Williamson to start a successful business, working with some of the same people she had worked *for* during her time in the corporate world. She took the key final step of putting her realization into action.

In contrast, Williamson also shared an experience where *not* fully understanding where her mind and heart were and whether they aligned to the point of commitment led her to being fired. She had worked in the beauty industry for many years and was then offered the role of head of marketing for a hair dye company, run by Hayley Williams, the lead singer of Paramore. She would be selling magenta, green, and purple hair dye, which was not on brand for Williamson.

"I wasn't being hired to be a cover model. I was being hired to develop new products and do the packaging and manage the vendors... That's my wheelhouse and I've done a lot of that," Williamson recognized, but she was fired for all of the red flags she had chosen to ignore from the start of accepting this role. She had wanted so badly for everything to work out, taking a job that on paper looked good because it was in her field. But she knew there were other expectations, influences, and red flags that didn't sit right. "I knew in my gut it wasn't right, and it ended up as a train wreck," she recalls.

Again, recognize why you are in the roles you have taken. Apply yourself in the direction that allows you to fulfill that purpose.

In Leonora Zilkha Williamson's life, at this point, everything is going right. She points out it is because she is constantly questioning whether her actions match what she really wants to be doing, and this never steers her in the wrong direction. Getting fired was difficult for her and resulted in a dramatic career shift, but what if she never got fired, never took the leap of faith, and was still sitting in corporate trainings wishing to be the trainer?

For many, the search for meaning takes on a more important role as they age, and the resulting tie to wellbeing is stronger. However, it must be done in a positive way, and there is often a source of prompting (Steger, Oishi and Kashdan, 2009). For Williamson, it was being fired; for others, it may be a challenge of sorts, like Boaz.

When it comes down to it, finding purpose is an elusive subject. It is personal, unique, requires you to exit your comfort zone, and has you push past your current reality. Once you have established your thought process, you can act. The component of authenticity that plays into this is making sure our actions not only are moral, standing by other values outside of the realms of curiosity and generosity, but also stand solidly within the medium of authenticity. When an action is authentic, there is an added layer of depth to our realities. It is something that on a subconscious level works with us, instead of against us.

Think BIG. There are no right or wrong answers, only your personal ones. If it helps, think about it this way: You should *want* to do things, rather than *have* to do them. The only things you really *have* to do fall exactly on the first tier of Maslow's hierarchy of basic human needs. You need to eat, sleep, and have shelter. That is pretty much it. Anything built on top of that, especially as you progress up the ladder, is a desire. It is absolutely imperative these desires are built on authentic thoughts—founded on your "why."

VISUALIZE YOUR "WHY" IN ACTION

Everything you can imagine is real.

—PABLO PICASSO

Have you ever watched someone else really enjoy an activity, and marvel at the intricacies of the work? Then you think, "Wow, I can never do that!"

My favorite pastime while I am at home is to watch my mother cook in the kitchen. She is very efficient with her process: setting up water to boil, cutting up raw vegetables, starting the soup, and then beginning to fry potatoes. It all makes sense in her head. It's a beautiful image for me, and every time is a fascinating new method that seems to end with even tastier food.

Every time, I end up walking away, shaking my head at the possibility of having to make soup, salad, pasta, rice, buckwheat, potatoes, chicken, and dessert for dinner, only to have to do it again the following day. This is a lack of ability to visualize. It never worked, and I thought

I was broken. I couldn't cook. My brother, who is six years younger than me, was better at making eggs than I was.

It was not until I moved to college and was forced to make my own food that I could even fathom the thought of standing by the stove to make myself a full meal. Suddenly, it was real.

In the context of authenticity, even if you have found your purpose in life, your true "why," it is nothing without the power of visualization. You need to be able to visualize yourself doing the action, or there will be no action. A 2006 documentary titled *The Secret* explores the power of thinking, among which is the power of visualization. It all starts with thinking about the life you want to live, but not in the way we've traditionally been taught. Imagine yourself ten years from now, doing what you want to be doing. It is *you* in the front line, the main character, the writer of your own tale, and the driver of all actions, no one else. Once you can visualize it, you can materialize it.

The key is to see yourself in the role. You are the protagonist. You are the main character.

In high school, I had a very close friend who was absolutely terrible in the lab. When we would come into our Research class, you could tell he was already miserable. What made matters worse was the second half of the course was entirely student driven. You had to pick a topic, design an experiment, and start working to produce substantial results you can base conclusions off by the end of the semester. The best projects would be selected to go to the local competition, from which it was possible to be selected each round for the Regeneron International Science and Engineering Fair.

For the first few weeks of the project, this friend and I sat around. We toyed with the idea of experimenting with cucumbers, which we as high school students found hilarious, and then moved on to more serious ideas. For his project, he finally settled on the different types of coffee and their antibacterial effects. The next step was to design an experiment, and he was the main comedian in the classroom. After doing his calculations, he proudly came up to the teacher, and announced he would need 500 to 1,000 Petri dishes, each with eight sections. A Petri dish is simply a small circle where you place the sample, and then you grow the bacteria in an incubator to see how much growth there is. The teacher, who was known for always keeping her cool, barely lifted a brow.

"Why don't you look over that math there? That doesn't sound right. What are you even doing?"

He looked at her, shot me a look across the room, and then looked back at her with puppy dog eyes. "I have no idea, and this is *so* not my thing."

The teacher, with little to no reaction, sent him back to his desk. "I'm not your babysitter or your mom to do basic math with you. We already learned all the skills you need to know for this experiment, especially yours. Look at your notes."

These were not the words he needed to hear, so he came over, pleading that I look over his work. We quickly figured out his mistake, and he finished the day off with, "I am never going to need this crap in the court room. Why am I spending my time on this?"

The next few months were full of lost coffee, overgrown bacteria, incomprehensible data, and a seemingly non-existent effort on his part. The worst part is I had *never,* and still haven't, seen him try harder. But, every day, he would walk out of the lab absolutely thrilled he was done for the day, and one hour closer to his career as a lawyer.

Do you see the problem here? He could not see himself in the role. He couldn't thrive as a student working in the lab because he could not visualize himself doing this. That was his only problem, especially given the resources available to him and the training he had prior to starting experimentation. In my friend's case, he was constantly sending out negative energy. Walking into the lab, he was in a state of annoyance, anger, and sadness. The project wasn't working, he wasn't good at lab work, and whatever else he could think of were all used as excuses.

If you can't imagine yourself doing something, you probably won't be able to.

Visualization has effects on a physical level. Olympic athletes constantly use as a way to practice and mentally prepare; they place themselves in a mental state of being at the event: they are running, skiing, swimming, etc. (Clarey, 2014). They are fully there, imagining themselves crossing the finish line and winning the highly coveted medal. When preparing for the Sochi Olympics, Canadian bobsledder Rosh would think about the course every morning, whether it be in the shower or while brushing his teeth. "It just takes a minute, so I do the whole thing or sometimes just the corners that are more technical. You try to keep it fresh in your head, so when you do get there, you are not just starting at square one. It's amazing how much you can do in your mind," he says about the experience.

American aerialist Emily Cook talks about her experiences with visualization in a different way, specifically her procedure of first recording the day step-by-step: standing on the hill, feeling the wind on her body, and hearing the crowd's energy. With each additional sense, there is a buildup to the visualization, and she begins the routine.

"I turn down the in-run. I stand up. I engage my core. I look at the top of the jump... I was going through every little step of how I wanted that jump to turn out," she says. When this recording is played back to her, she comments on her muscles tightening in the right moments, almost like she was there. Long term, it made her significantly more prepared for the actual day of the competition. She was already mentally there, and all she had to do was physically match that preparation.

The most impressive part of visualization comes from the muscular response to the imagining the experience: when a high physical performer uses the power of visualization, the movements are registered in the brain the same way they would if they were actually performed, and brain has the same response. As a result, the neural network is fired up in the same way as it would if someone was actually performing that activity, and the muscles are engaged to a nearly exact degree. This is a concept explored by Psychoneuromuscular Theory and applies to the common individual in the same way as it would to an athlete. If you can clearly visualize yourself in the role, then you can train yourself to get to the final result. If you cannot even imagine yourself in the role, it will make it exceptionally difficult for that to happen (Cleere, 2012).

Your attitude, mindset, and emotions are key to the effectiveness of your visualization techniques.

Omar Alshogre tells a story about how this ability to visualize gave him the power to survive, and eventually speak and share his story in TED Talk format. Alshogre is a twenty-six-year-old Syrian refugee who had been arrested at the age of fifteen for joining a rally protesting the government. He was thrown in prison for what would become one of seven prison experiences, the last of which came at seventeen and lasted for three years. Prison in Syria is very different to that in the US. In stark contrast to even the worse treatment in US prisons, Syrian prisoners, each of whom were given a forty-centimeter by forty-centimeter square, had a strict schedule: wake up, go through between one to four hours of torture, use the bathroom, eat a little food, and then return to your room. In your room, there was not enough space for everyone to sit, so people would alternate, four hours of sitting, then four hours of standing, constantly shifting.

Throughout his time in the prison, Alshogre created a life for himself. It was through visualization he was able to place himself outside of his body during beatings. By understanding the ultimate goal is survival while being able to enjoy what could possibly be the last years of his life, he lived long enough to share his story. He had his "why."

The "how" came as he spent more time in prison. He knew the values he had been taught as a child: respect, kindness, generosity. He needed to live through this experience without losing himself. He visualized himself free, eating a full meal, back with his family.

If you find your why and are able to imagine yourself doing it, you are golden.

When Omar Alshogre shared this story in his TED Talk, he spoke in English. He knew this was worth explaining to people, clarifying the mental and physical terrors Syrians in prison go through. He explained everything in painful detail, reliving his trauma with every word. He was finally able to fulfill his mission which he had determined in prison. Visualization had gotten him there, and now he was using the power of visualization to place the audience in his shoes.

I spoke to him and asked him about the talk, commenting on how well he was able to connect with the audience and the confidence in his speech. "You definitely can't imagine. I didn't speak English! I memorized every single word. Really, every single word. I had done that! I didn't know what I was saying, but I knew it was really fun." With that, he ran to his next meeting. I was shocked. I rewatched the video and still could not tell the talk was memorized.

I, as the listener, did not know. The listeners in the room did not know. He had entered the stage with complete confidence, faked it, and absolutely made it. His future then materialized before him, opening up numerous opportunities for him to help those in similar situations, such as speaking in front of the US Senate, serving as the Director of Detainees Affairs, working at the Boston Consulting Group (BCG), and attending Georgetown University.

To some degree, visualizing confidence is almost tricking your brain into believing you can do it. The phrase "fake it 'til you make it" is more founded than you might realize. The same way taking risks makes it easier to take risks, feigning confidence will make you more confident. This is due to the Hebbian Principle, which states two actions done together will become interlinked (Shukla, 2018). The more you do an action purposefully to see a certain effect, the more you will see the effect. With each time, the purposeful action becomes easier, and the effect comes quicker.

No one can tell you're faking it but you.

Clearly, it works. By building on reality and visualizing yourself in some higher state than where you are at this point in time, you improve your future. The best way to have a solid foundation is to take your current situation, add in your habits and talents, and think up the best-case scenario for the future.

In the case of Jeffrey Seller, numerous talents in the realm of producing allowed him to find his role as a leader early on and then apply them to the musical theatre industry, specifically.

Seller describes his progress in the theatre industry as steady. It was a classic case of climbing the ladder one rung at a time. Around the age of eight or nine, he saw a high school production of an original rock musical based on Rumpelstiltskin. He was inspired. The musical took him to a place he had never been before, both aurally and from a storytelling point of view. Seller was intrigued by the notion of taking a story he already knew, Rumpelstiltskin, and translating it into a contemporary work.

Shortly after, his temple was doing an annual Purim play, and they had a very creative director who would juxtapose the story of Queen Esther with a preexisting Broadway musical or story. Seller auditioned and was placed in the chorus because he did not yet know how to read speeches or prepare for auditions. He had never done something like this before! That was his official introduction to the musical theatre world, and not soon after he was sitting in class and started writing a play. *Adventureland* became the title of the full play Seller wrote at the time, and in fifth grade, following some time given by the teacher to workshop it, he directed it and performed it with all his friends.

Seller's talent was officially unlocked: He had started producing, directing, and conceiving shows. By seventh grade, he was doing community theatre and youth theatre. In high school, he was competing in the high school shows with the Thespian Society events that every state does and producing the spring pops concerts. He was raising money selling local businesses ads in programs, and in his local youth theater he became the chairman of the play reading committee and started picking the plays.

At its core, though, the talent was innate leadership. According to Seller, he has a macro mind. He looks at the big picture and can see how systems should be run. He has always been able to do so because he is a big idea person with a natural inclination toward leadership.

"The job of a producer is to build a show that in success will be exploited for many years to come in cities all over the country and perhaps all over the world," he pointed out.

If it is your calling, you'll likely apply the skills associated with it in more ways than one.

If Seller had not gone into producing, he might be in politics, as his college major suggested. The macro issues of building alliances between countries and settling international conflicts were points of interest for him.

"Producers produce their lives. They know how to make stuff happen. and they know how to think ahead to tomorrow, next week, next month. I know how to plan ahead," he described.

This is a talent that was inherently innate, Seller argued, but it was also built upon and practiced. From a young age, he was given ample opportunities to lead in his community, including a successful neighborhood camp he organized in fifth grade.

In his career, one thing was clear: He had discovered his talents. Everything made sense from there, and he was able to begin practicing. Once the talent is identified, it is much easier to produce work that is convincing and well put-together.

> *Our habits and talents are helpful hints to what our "why" might be and make it easier to visualize a future.*

Mikel Ellcessor is an individual who has applied his talents in radio hosting to his mission. Specifically, he points out his abilities come from his ability to embrace appropriate levels of vulnerability in the work setting. This intrinsically lies in a willingness to become known or a willingness to let people get to know him. Although not a talent in the traditional sense, it is certainly a skill that has helped him advance significantly in his career and has been very useful for the companies he has been a part of.

"It is a willingness to be candid and say the hard thing, or just to ask the hard question," he pointed out. There are always things people want to avoid but getting into the aspects of conversation people tend to skirt around is what Mikel excels at. In his time studying with the Jesuits, he found immense impact from their teachings. They stressed a synthesized world view, bringing in literature and science, spirituality, and a sense of curiosity, all of which allowed him to develop applicable skills around reading, writing, and critical thought. There was a clear talent on his part for recognizing the hard questions and being able to ask them, and then the teaching allowed him to build on this talent with habit, with the whole mind thinking approach being truly foundational to making good strategies, good organizational development, and good planning. He is able to take in different views and perspectives, making him a clearly valuable addition to the company.

Mikel's background further explains the origins of his talents. Growing up in a multiethnic environment, working on job sites with his dad, people came from various backgrounds (racial, socioeconomic, etc.), and living in South Africa during the apartheid years influenced his current actions. Rather than using this ability to ask hard questions in a way similar to a litigation lawyer, his focus was turned elsewhere: diversity and inclusion, specifically in the entertainment business. That is why the many years he spent in public radio were focused on discussions about why media makers, as community builders and people who had a service orientation, need to address this. It was a candid conversation, with little results.

With the recent cultural shift to truly reward the inclusion of BIPOC in all spaces, Mikel has learned to use his talent and pivot. Now, it is not just a willingness to be open and have difficult conversations. It is also a willingness to think about things differently, to stretch. He recognizes there is absolutely no need to pursue perfection, but simply a willingness to embrace the process of change and growth.

The takeaway from Mikel's story? A talent can be absolutely anything. It is something that is ingrained from a young age and shaped by your experiences. Most importantly, it needs to be built on. Without reinforcement, even the strongest walls can be easily toppled.

Identifying talents can help you visualize yourself in the role. You still need to work on reinforcing those talents so you do not become complacent.

The importance of reinforcement shows up in interesting ways, namely when researching routine (Arlinghaus and Johnston, 2019). During the summer months, when children lack structure, they gain weight. Families with a bedtime routine will have improved functioning and sleep habits. Routines are also attributed to social skill development, academic success, and resilience in crisis. Those successful at weight loss have an eating schedule without skipped meals. The reasoning behind this: habit formation.

Another was to think about this as "practice makes perfect." The 10,000-hour rule, referenced and popularized by Malcolm Gladwell in his book *Outliers*, states 10,000 hours of practice are required for mastery of any skill or material.

The concept of reinforcement is something I am all too familiar with. When I was younger, there was only one subject I struggled in: writing (ironic, huh?). I would have above a 95 percent on every quiz and test, in every subject, and then come home with one 80 percent on my report card. I just couldn't do it. My sentence structure and grammar followed all the rules, I followed the directions, but I just could not nail what my teachers asked of me.

In third grade, I had a teacher named Mrs. Zanga. To this day, this is one of the most influential teachers and mentors in my life because she killed with kindness, and she killed my report card with an 80 percent for writing. She would work me hard in class and challenge me in a way no other teachers I had up to that point did, and for the majority of my schooling would. She asked the hard questions and pushed me to keep practicing. "Recognizing the perfectionism I exhibited in my work, she granted me opportunities to rewrite anything I wanted to for a better grade because she wanted me to improve."

"Just imagine, you could be a writer someday!" she told me, and I laughed at the notion.

When third grade ended, I declared I was never writing again. It was too hard, and I spent too much time on it. So, my parents got me a writing tutor. A sarcastic "yippee!" was all I can say about how I felt when I heard this news. Twice a week for two to three hours, I met with Masha. Every week, I'd pump out four to five full writing pieces, each time taking less and less time to do it, with the work becoming more coherent, concise, well-written, and relevant to the questions at hand.

In eighth grade, I received a 100 percent on a writing assignment from the strictest teacher in the school. In eleventh, my reading and writing teacher praised me for my work. Now, I am writing a book. Something that once felt foreign, strange, difficult, unnecessary, and annoying is now second nature. It feels right, and I can spend hours at a time typing away or writing out a journal to clear my head. Something clicked: talent unlocked + hard work forced + passion discovery in process + visualization of possible ending.

Combine your talents with the hard work of improving them, and as long as you are working on a passion, you should be able to visualize your self-actualized future self.

The best part is it is never too late to visualize your "why" in action. Every talent you have been given can be used, usually to serve something greater than yourself and to improve the world around you.

For Ed Bacon, visualization played a major role in his spiritual journey to fulfilling his purpose.

At the age of five or six, Bacon was in a grove of pine trees in South Georgia when all of a sudden he was surrounded by light, warmth, and wisdom. An inaudible voice said to him, "You are the most special, wonderful person I ever made, and everyone else, too." The message was clear: Everyone was created equal. The society Bacon had grown up in as a white male in the South was one of a hierarchy, with the Baptist Church he was a part of looking down on non-Christians, people of color, and the LGBTQ community. This became the roadmap for the rest of Bacon's life.

Bacon went to college, where he had no idea what he was supposed to study. He was a social butterfly, president of numerous organizations, and very active in campus politics. Some suggested he go into ministry, but this was not a possibility for him because of the hierarchies his religion presented. Others recommended he attend law school where he had another mystical experience.

It was the final exam for the Uniform Commercial Codes class, and Bacon knew the material backwards and forwards. He spent the first two hours outlining his response, and then went outside to take a break. It was snowing lightly, a romantic scene, as he described it.

Here came the inaudible voice again, the first time since Bacon was a little kid.

"Are you an attorney?" the voice asked.

Bacon said no. He couldn't see himself as such.

"If you are not an attorney, do you need a law degree?" the voice said.

Bacon responded with a no.

"If you do not need a law degree, do you need to finish this exam?" was the final question.

No.

Bacon walked out, leaving everything on the desk. He called his now-wife very excitedly, "You will not believe what I just did... I quit law school!" To say the least, she was not happy, but they figured it out. They moved to Mercer University, where he served as the campus minister. His father and a board of deacons ordained him, making him a Baptist minister, and Bacon was able to work there for a few years.

This was the end of law school! The power of visualization was not working, and he could not do it. There was no future in the law for Bacon, and regardless of how far he had come, there would be no point in continuing to pursue someone else's passion. It was time for him to visualize a new, more passion-founded future.

Soon enough, Bacon recognized he could not serve the very sect that the voice's message went against. Another point of inflection occurred, and he fell in love with the Episcopal Church, to which he converted and became an Episcopal minister.

"I was dishonoring my family by converting, doing things that were impossible. But I had a moment of clarity, and I knew that I am an Episcopal minister. I am not a Baptist minister," he explained, going into depth about the issues within the family, and to his mental health, that this life-changing decision caused.

Since then, Bacon had a very successful career in Episcopal ministry. The reason he was able to do this? He recognized the path he was on was not one he could visualize himself pursuing.

It is never too late to find your "why" and begin visualizing a life that is realistic given your talents and habits.

The takeaway here is your opportunities are limitless. Our brains can easily be tricked into thinking a different reality exists, and it is your job to take advantage of this. Find a future you can clearly visualize, and then make sure it is one founded on your "why." Your habits and talents are likely going to play into that—after all, there's a reason you do them so much, right?

ALIGN YOUR "HOW" TO CREATE SYNERGY

He who has a why to live for can bear almost any how.

—NIETZCHE

What do you day to day? How have those habits translated into hobbies? How have they changed your identity? Does this fit into your "why"? Can you visualize a future?

The final key to living your most authentic self is aligning your "how" to your "why" and creating a synergy that feels natural. A person who truly aligns their answers to these questions will self-actualize because they are moving forward; a person who pushes a life that lacks alignment will feel unmotivated, and even mentally or physically ill.

According to Gestalt's Theory of Personality, behavior is a result of the person and their environment. The entire ecosystem is investigated to get a better sense of how the organism fits in (Burley, 2012). An individual aligning their "how" with their "why" is the only one who will function harmoniously.

Jason Nelson learned this the hard way. In college, there were two versions of him. There was the business student attending marketing classes, during which he would put on his headphones and DJ for fun. Then there was the recording arts student version of Jason, where content covered included royalties and copyrights, production, and recording. During these, Jason was busy applying to business and marketing jobs. There was a hint of purpose but no alignment internally for how to get there.

The thing about Jason is he is *incredibly* musically talented. He has perfect pitch and can play any song by ear on either the piano or the saxophone. Up to this point, though, his "why" had been the cliche business undergraduate degree, future marriage to a nice girl, and then starting a family. Not a hint of Jason or his personality in Jason's life plan, and it certainly wasn't working.

"I felt like Troy Bolton from *High School Musical*. I was in two different worlds, and I would look around me and see overflowing passion from my peers. They would lock themselves in a room and produce music for thirteen hours, then go to bed at 4:00 a.m. I just didn't see the appeal, and I thought there was something wrong with me," Nelson reflected, adding that he preferred interacting with peers at more social activities, like football games or other gatherings where you could feel the energy in the air. One thing was clear. Jason Nelson was meant to be a performer, working in the music business and interacting with people on the daily.

On March 23, 2019, Jason Nelson's life changed. He was hired to perform piano at his friend's sister's wedding cocktail hour, and suddenly, the world was his oyster. It was time to take action. One look at the deteriorating and out-of-tune piano at home was enough of a realization that things needed to change. Nelson bought himself a nice keyboard and started to practice every day, preparing songs that would give off the right energy for a party.

At the wedding, Nelson also ended up playing the sax with the DJ, and he realized he wanted to combine his ability to play the saxophone by ear along with his passion for seeking out high-energy environments. That is why this wedding was a life-changer. The insecurities associated with comparing his abilities to those of professional performers drifted away. He got dressed up, headed over to the closest park, and took some promo pics he sent around to DJs in the area in an effort to promote his services and gain experience.

Every day, his discipline grew. With each new gig he was getting, he realized this was an untapped market, and not only was he following his "why," but the "how" was finally falling into place. Now, two and a half years since he started working in the industry and a little over a year since he left his full-time job, he realizes this is the start of something new. Nelson is living on his own, paying his own bills, and fills his time with his passion for music and energy.

Jason Nelson is the epitome of alignment. He found his purpose, and then acted on it. There are two components to being successful in an action: talents and habits. When they both produce a green light, there will be continuous positive feedback on your end with the action, and you will want to continue doing/participating in it. Any one is simply not enough.

> *Once you've found your why, act on it. Do so by utilizing your talents, and then building habits that improve on those talents.*

The talents are things you are good at naturally. These are your potentialities. If you develop these talents through hard work (namely with good habits), you can get very far. Without developing those habits, it is unlikely the talent will go anywhere. A talent can be a quick grasp of numbers. There is lots of potential there, and by doing math problems that challenge you, you can advance through to questions of higher complexity.

When I was younger, my "talent" was piano. Every day for the majority of my childhood, I practiced the pieces I was working on, prepared for the competitions months ahead, and created programs for performances or examinations coming up. I dreaded sitting down in front of the instrument, and from the age of five to thirteen, I regularly thought about burning it down.

My hard work was something that made my parents proud of me, though, and every time we had guests come over, everyone would sit down and listen to me play for around half an hour. The piano room was filled with thirty/forty-something-year-olds around my parents age, enjoying the classical works I had practiced that month. When they got bored, they would walk over to me, praise me for all my hard work, tell me how amazing it was I was practicing so much, and how talented I was, and then leave the room to get some dinner.

Their praise made it seem worth it. Reassurance from others always meant a lot to me and getting acknowledgment for my efforts from such a large quantity of people kept me going. Outside of that, I knew I was an above-average performer. I worked hard and had achieved a variety of awards for my playing, but there was no future between me and piano after high school graduation.

There was something missing. There was talent. There was hard work. Abilities + habits = success? Nope. There was no alignment, like Jason has. Performing classical music did not fill me up, energize me, or drive me forward. Everything was there on paper, my "what" and "how" were figured out, but the "why" was nowhere to be found.

Just because you are talented and build habits that could make you successful on paper does not mean you will be happy doing them. They need to match your "why."

Just having healthy habits, and even enormous amounts of hard work, will never compare to the effect of having both the raw talent and the hard work built on top of passion. In my experience playing piano, I have never been the best because it wasn't my dream. It did not matter how many hours a day I would practice or what the piece

I was playing was (in terms of how well it matched my personality and skills). The hard work was present, the commitment was as well, for over a decade. However, these were the foundation, and the passion never came.

When I came to college, I became exposed to individuals who were truly talented in their musical careers and had become uber successful due to their impeccable work ethics. One of these individual, Akash Gururaja is a peer who plays both the piano and violin, has perfect pitch, and produces music for Gold Revere, recently signed by Sony. *That* is talent. He can play all the same things I can and was trained with the same classical training I was. The difference: passion.

For Lissy Wood, a current junior studying chemistry at Vanderbilt, the three questions of how, why, and what aligned, and she saw success in her work because of it. Her "why" from a young age has been understanding the world around her through the scientific method. In high school, she was highly interested in the hard sciences, so she chose her classes accordingly. Her sophomore year, she realized she had already taken the difficult courses offered and made the decision to leave high school early and apply to an early college program. Lissy ended up attending Bard College, where she again was taking courses that didn't challenge her mentally. She easily aced the courses supposedly meant to weed out students lacking in ability or dedication. She committed herself to finding a lab to work in, but there were minimal research opportunities available, which is the career Lissy plans to pursue. After the second year, due to not having enough of a challenge for her research abilities, she transferred to Vanderbilt.

At first, she did not feel comparable to the other students, but quickly she recognized something: There were always going to be students who take five minutes to see something and get the answer, and others have to work at things for hours. The end result was usually the same: As and Bs. Even though Lissy had come in with a strong talent for research, she was still challenged by this new environment, and her talent was no longer going to be enough.

This meant she had to work harder, building new habits that would allow her to continue to succeed. This is a common struggle students face because they don't have a built-in system for effective study habits (Bahrami Susan et al., 2011). Wood has been successful in doing so, receiving a research grant for the summer following her first year at Vanderbilt, and continuing to work in a laboratory environment numerous times a week, utilizing principles of electrochemistry to create a bio-hybrid solar cell device using photosynthetic proteins extracted from spinach.

Habits are defined as automatic actions, triggered as a response to contextual cues. With each repetition of the action, the association between the cue and the response is solidified, and it becomes a more cognitively efficient process, meaning the conscious attention and dependence on a motivational process reduces, and you have to do less thinking to get it done (Gardner, 2012). For example, if you are trying to drink more water, you could start with associating drinking water with waking up. Waking up acts as a cue, then you would consciously make the choice to drink water, the action. After about eighteen repetitions, you will instinctually wake up and reach for the water (Arlinghaus and Johnston, 2019).

The same thing occurs on a higher level. Studying for a new subject requires a different method, which is at first difficult. With each time it is done, it gets easier. Working on our talents is the same. Talents are skills that come naturally but need to be honed. This is done through effective habits and hard work. Forming these habits is easier if they align with your purpose.

Create habits that allow you to practice and enhance your skills or talents.

The importance of alignment shines through in Pritesh Shah's story, one that combines many of the themes in this book: purpose, values, and specifically abilities and talents. Shah went to college pursuing a major in accounting and a minor in English, with the initial goal of attending law school after graduation. He was killing it in school; he was working hard, things were relatively easy for him, and he was very involved in extracurricular activities. As the VP of the Accounting Society, he was all in.

That was until an Indian guru came to him home and read his astrological chart.

"What do you want to do? What are you going to school for?" the guru asked.

"Accounting," Shah responded. This was met with laughter, so as to say, "There's not a chance you will ever use that degree." Shah left this conversation angry. He thought this meant he would be homeless.

A year and a half later, Shah graduated from college, and there were about six more months until he would start working. His mom had found an ad in the newspaper for a commercial acting class about an hour and a half down from where they lived. Shah did not plan on sitting at home and doing nothing, so he decided to go for it. It would be fun, something to do on the side.

The teacher told him that he was talented and connected him with an agent. Before he knew it, Shah was at an audition and then signed. It felt good. It was something he wanted to do.

Then, June started to creep up. It was time to start the new job, and Shah had to begin preparing to go to work. Part of that preparation was getting a physical with the doctor. His doctor was unamused.

"He kind of stared at me for a second, and then said, 'You know, most people are pretty excited for their first job. You're not excited at all.' and I responded, 'It's just a job.'" In the meantime, Shah was booking print gigs, and doing little things here and there, absolutely loving his new life.

A lack of alignment is something you will feel physically and emotionally. You might feel more tired, depressed, burnt out. All of these suggest what you are doing may not be for you.

Before he knew it, June rolled around. It was the Friday before Shah was supposed to go to work, and he was freaking out. He was crying, having panic attacks, and everything in his heart was saying, "You can't take this job." Shah called human resources at the firm, and no one answered. He left a voicemail saying he would not be able to come in on Monday because he had figured out what he wants to do with his life. A couple of hours later, a lady from HR calls him back and says, "'Honey, I wish I did that when I was your age. Go kill it."

Since then, Shah has worked on numerous projects, among them advertisements with Caitlyn Jenner. He is entirely self-sufficient living in Hollywood.

In his case, there were talents on both ends: He was excelling in school, doing well in his accounting classes, and fully capable of continuing to work in the field. Capable did not mean willing. That is where habits and mindset come in. Purpose-driven individuals sometimes forget to think with their hearts, and that is exactly what Pritesh Shah avoided doing in this situation. He is now incredibly happy with his career.

Living an aligned life can seem daunting but starting is often the most difficult part. Be generous, courageous, and authentic in your actions.

Thus, the core elements of living a realistic mission are tied with our abilities. Each and every person is born with talents—this can be a communication style, a leadership strategy, a musical skill, or an inclination toward STEM. Whatever it may be, it is important to recognize it and begin building on it. The earlier this is done, the more practice and wisdom will come of it, and the greater long-tern impact you can make.

For Don North, it was less of a talent, and more of an inclination toward education. He lives by the words of Margaret Mead, "A clear understanding of the problem prefigures the lines of its solution." For North, the problem in college was that he had no idea what he wanted to do following graduation. He was attending Vanderbilt on a football scholarship, enjoyed sports, and really loved to read, so he majored in English. The spring of his senior year, he got a phone call from a fraternity brother teaching at a Boys School in Dallas. They were looking for an English teacher and a football coach! Thus began a career of what North describes as luck, but truly a natural alignment between talent, hard work, and a job that matched his purpose.

"I was thinking I'd do this for a couple of years and then do what grownups are supposed to do. Law school, medical school, business school, and get some kind of real job," North commented. The alignment was something North couldn't shake, though, and actually struggled with for the first few years on the job. It took him about three years to leave behind the feelings of guilt about how much fun he was having.

> *Doing something that aligns with your purpose will, and should, feel natural. It should be challenging but fun.*

"I thought work was supposed to be something you did to earn a living, support your family. Work, work, work. Work and fun aren't supposed to be in the same ballpark, and I literally felt guilty about enjoying my work until I just decided, you know, maybe it's okay to really like what you're doing," North described, and elaborated on why he felt teaching was his passion.

He found in both teaching and coaching, there would come an "aha!" moment when a student in his class or an athlete he was coaching would figure out how to do something they didn't quite understand before. There were times of increased pride, excitement, and confidence, and part of it could be attributed to the mentor. In this case that was him, and he found it difficult to turn his back on that and declare he was done, ready to try something else.

The people around North also recognized the alignment between his purpose and his work, because at twenty-five, he was promoted to the chairman of the English Department, affirming his feeling that this might possibly be a career. A few years later, the mother of one of his students told him that he would be headmaster one day—planting the seed.

Eventually, North was middle school principal, then upper school principal, and finally head of the school. For the next decades of his life, there would be constant progression, and because he was acting in line with his purpose, things felt *right*. Looking back, it seems like there was a logical path, like he planned it from the beginning, and this was his goal all along. Clearly, this could not be further from the truth. Instead, he took the time to explore the problem at hand, and then the solution came through with time.

The key to all of this is perspective. Things will change, but that is important for you to be able to find your true alignment.

When I spoke to serial entrepreneur Carlo Navarro, the importance of coming to terms with change and the failure that comes with it was something he emphasized. His most recent idea is more of a personal challenge to get back into a sport for which he had discovered a natural talent at an early age, but never pursued.

> *It is never too late to switch things up for better alignment.*

Navarro played golf for the very first time in eighth grade, when he went out to the golf course with his uncle on Easter. He scored a fifty, an impressive score for a first-time player. After that round, Navarro and his uncle were so excited! They stopped at the golf store and bought a set of clubs.

The clubs stood in the garage without being touched until Navarro's junior year of high school when he decided to try out for the school golf team. Surprise: He made the team! He played that summer every day, getting better and better with each practice. After that year, the golf clubs again retired to the garage, for about twenty years.

COVID-19 brought a comeback for golf in Navarro's life. His four kids were going stir-crazy and needed to get out, so he decided to take them golfing. Out of all possibilities, golf was one of the only options available during the lockdowns. They got out the clubs, sat down in the car, and drove to the local golf course. The kids were so excited, and the day reignited Navarro's love for golf.

As they were driving around the course in a cart, they were able to let loose. The kids were laughing, screaming out of the cart, and there was a sense of normalcy many were hoping to get during the COVID-19 lockdown. A thought went through Navarro's head, "I was looking back at it, and I could have been good at it. Why didn't I pursue this?"

That day created a greater alignment for Navarro with the sport. The family needed this outing, and there was a channel for them to open up and express themselves. It wasn't even about golf specifically, but about bringing his kids together and setting an example for them. Why couldn't Navarro pursue this?

He set a new goal for himself: to become a professional player. The reasoning wouldn't be what you expect. At this point in his life, Navarro aims to lead by example for his children, and show them how to live life in a way that promotes a sense of self, rather than tell them. The cliche "Chase your dreams!" doesn't work, and he wanted to give them a more concrete example. He wanted to show them if he fails, he fails greatly, so they can say, "Ny dad thought he would become a professional golfer," and whether Navarro is successful or not, this is a lesson the kids can take away. It is okay to fail. There are so many new things to learn, and it doesn't necessarily have anything to do with the initial goal you may present yourself with.

"Talent is everywhere, but opportunity is not. I want to encourage my children to learn from the opportunities they have, and I can do so through my own pursuits and passions. I am showing them it is okay to change your dreams and support multiple ones," he points out.

Navarro is teaching his kids a very important lesson: Alignment does not always come naturally, but it is important to be honest with yourself because sometimes the ideal scenario just will not pan out. This is why the average person has about twelve jobs in a span of thirty-two years, why 55 percent of Americans expect to search for a new job in the next year, why 30 percent of people work only to get them by (Bureau of Labor Statistics, Foster, 2021, Pew Research). It is why entrepreneurs are largely unsuccessful, with 90 percent of startups failing, 21.5 percent of which fail within the first year, 30 percent within the second, 50 percent within the third, and 70 percent in their tenth (Bryant, 2020). Failure is going to occur, and we must learn to love it. It is an indication you are one step closer to finding alignment and creating the necessary synergy to self-actualize.

At the end of the day, we all have our talents, hard work, and our passions. When these three come together, it's like magic. Things become easier to do because they feel natural. It is no longer an expectation of you to do something, and instead is an opportunity to learn and grow, bringing you further in your personal growth. Alignment allows for a truly self-actualized form of yourself to shine through.

TL; DR

Passion is energy. Feel the power that comes from focusing on what excites you.

—OPRAH WINFREY

The key takeaway from the value of authenticity is there is truly nothing in this world worth your time unless you give it 100 percent. Your all or nothing because half-assing something is going to waste your time and energy, annoy the people around you, and hold you back from achieving your truest and fullest potential.

- While you search for your why, act according to your values. These will ensure you are the best version of yourself when you've found your purpose.
- You should be able to visualize yourself living a life with your chosen "purpose"; it should feel natural.
- Once you have found your why, align your actions to it. Build your life around it. Be purposeful about where you spend your time and energy.
- You do not *have* to do anything. Avoid relying on goals to cure a lack of passion; instead, go and try things until they feel right.

- When an action is authentic, there is an added layer of depth to our realities. It is something that works with us on a subconscious level, instead of against us.

CONCLUSION

The journey to self-actualization will always be an uphill battle. A self-actualized six-year-old is not the same as a self-actualized sixty-year-old. The one consistent factor is there will always be a clear catalyst for the transformation that exists: for some, that may have been COVID-19, which gave you a moment to breathe, relax, and return to the self you love. For others, that may be grieving the loss of a close family member and realizing time is absolutely precious and valuable. For all of us, there is an external sense of expectations and assumptions, with everyone defining success for us. This needs to be an individual process.

It is like walking through complete darkness, in a jungle. As the sun starts to rise, you begin to see things more clearly: There are trees, animals, bodies of water. Maybe a path. With the light come answers, but additional awareness of challenges. Hunger, poisonous creatures, and swampy surfaces are all new problems you were not even remotely aware of during the night.

As you keep walking, you become distracted. There is a lawn with flowers, and like Dorothy, you become intoxicated by the poppy seed high. You become lost, and there needs to be something sharp to pull you out of that trance. Once you return to the forest, your mindset is forever changed because of the new experience you just had. Rather than continuing straight away, you may now stop to smell the flowers every time you see one.

For me, my journey toward self-actualization began with my loss of purpose. Slowly, through this book, and many, many experiences I have not enjoyed (and used to rule out potential purposes), I have been able to gain clarity. When I worked in the lab, my mentality was to "Go, go go! Finish things as quickly as possible to get out of here." With tutoring students, even though I may enjoy it, the clock ticking away the seconds before class is over is a delight.

On the other hand, I have found religion to be a consolation. Friday night Shabbat dinners provide structure. Discussions with religious leaders provide me with a different perspective, instill their wisdom in me, and expand my imagination of what is possible. There is a reason millions of people—billions over the last few hundred years—have followed various religions and traditions. Innate wisdom lies in the stories our families tell, behind our traditions, and an overwhelming positive energy comes from promoting better understanding yourself from within.

Even though I do not believe this is my purpose, I feel closer than ever before. It has given me a foundation for values I am proud to live by and build on. Each day is a new challenge and invitation to be better than the previous one, to be nicer, kinder, more patient. Each day, a vision for my future becomes clearer in my mind. It's almost like this:

I encourage you to find something that acts as the sunlight, something that will always be able to snap you out of whatever trance you may be in momentarily, and something that will add joy to your life. These are things that are whole and precious; hold on to them but be prepared for change. Be ready to mourn the losses that come with change—not in the traditional way, but in a form of acceptance.

Finally, believe in yourself. Apply an entrepreneurial mindset to your life. Make it *yours*, and live it. There's only one.

ACKNOWLEDGMENTS

I'd like to acknowledge those who have given this book, and the stories within it, legs strong enough to move forward:

Yuliana Kazhdan, Elinor Teper, The Kazhdan, Midlin, Yakobovich, Kripitser, Groysman, Goldberg, Orak, Gitelman, Friedman, Agajanov, Sheynkman, Rubinshteyn, and Gandelman Families, Mackenzie Horne, Lissy Wood, Simone Stoyen, Paul M. Kurtz, and Eric Koester.

I'd like to thank Shlomo and Nechama Rothstein, as well as Chana Gwinisch and Malka Meyers, for helping me find joy in the spiritual world and for giving me the guidance necessary to bring it to you in this book.

I'd like to give special thanks to Faiqa Zafar for her patience in editing my work and excellent recommendations.

I'd like to thank all the individuals who devoted their time to do an interview with me. This book would not exist without your wisdom and stories!

I'd also like to gratefully acknowledge all the people who believed in this dream and made publishing it a reality:

Abby Schwartz, Adam Matar, Adir Grant, Akash Gururaja, Alan Levy, Aleksey Ikhelson, Alex Midlin, Alex Sheyfer, Alex Yakobovich, Alexander Krasovitsky, Alla Friedman, Anastasia Ivanov, Anna Begelfer, Anna Costa, Anna Karminsky, Anna Kripitser, Arkadiy Gitelman, Arkady Berkovsky, Asher Alcobi, Boaz Arzi, Bob Bernstein, Boris Gedzberg, Boris Kripitser, Brandon Sirochinsky, Carol Silver, Charan Singh, Dalton Gullett, Daniel Shade, Dennis Goldberg, Dmitry Abramov, Dmitry Burshteyn, Dolcinea Carroll, Elinor Teper, Elisabeth Wood, Eric Koester, Erica Rankin, Eva Kharitonov, Galina Silver, Galo Bowen, Gili Inbar, Gulnara Rubinshteyn, Ilana Gitelman, Ilona Levy, Inna Dijour, Inna Kotsubey, Irina Efraimovich, Irina Mogilnitzky, Jared Bauman, John Chandler, Julia Bakshiyev, Julia Pesikov, Julia Suris, Juzel Lloyd, Karina Agajanov, Katarina Cohen, Katerina Ginberg, Kiron Sharma, Laila Khreisat, Lana Stepman, Laura Hook, Lev Karminsky, Levi Welton, Lori Benvenuto, Luba Sheynkman, Margarita Aronov, Maria Sedunova, Marina Vinnik, Marisa Boon, Mariya Ardashnikova, Mark Sapara, Marty Grady, Mason Range, Max Eleftherio, Michael Chokler, Miranda Sapoznik, Mohammad Shafaie, Natalia Carrillo, Natalya Kunina, Norm Dannen Jr., Nosa O., Oksana Villa, Oleg Perel, Oleg Vernik, Olga Gurin, Olga Landa, Olga Nisenboym, Olga Orak, Paul M. Kurtz, Peter Malek, Rachel Smith, Rashmi K. Drummond, Rina Granik, Robert A. Mayans, Robert Guzman, Ryan Arranz, Ryan Morris, Sasha Krasny, Sharon Stern Richardson, Shina Kim, Stella Fleyshmakher, Stephen Box, Svetlana Lyulka, Tatiana Fulton, Tatiana Zlotnikova, Tatyana Smertenko, Teresa Xu, Tokunbo Faparusi, Avi Vainshtein, Ettel Vainshtein, Vitaly Zabarskiy, Vlada Gershfeld, Whitney Austin, Yana

Razova, Yelena Kolosovskiy, Yelena Smelyanskiy, Yevgeniya Yakobovich, Yuliana Kazhdan, Yuliya Simonov, Zaneta Lukauskas, and Zhanna Anash.

APPENDIX

INTRODUCTION

Pew Research Center. *The State of American Jobs.* October, 2016. https://www.pewresearch.org/social-trends/wp-content/uploads/sites/3/2016/10/ST_2016.10.06_Future-of-Work_FINAL4-1.pdf.

DEFINING SELF-ACTUALIZATION

Dubov, Nissan Dovid. "What is Life's Purpose?" *Chabad.org News*, Accessed October 7, 2021. https://www.chabad.org/library/article_cdo/aid/108390/jewish/What-is-Lifes-Purpose.htm

Encyclopaedia Britannica Online. Academic ed. s.v. "Self-actualization." Accessed October 7, 2021, https://www.britannica.com/science/self-actualization.

Fox, Sharon E., Pat Levitt, and Charles A. Nelson. "How the Timing and Quality of Early Experiences Influence the Development of Brain Architecture." *Child Development* 81, no. 1 (2010): 28–40. https://doi.org/10.1111/j.1467-8624.2009.01380.x

Golstein, Kurt. *The Organism*. New York: Zone Books, 2000.

Ismail, Nik and Mustafa Tekke. "Rediscovering Rogers's Self Theory and Personality." *Journal of Education, Health and Community Psychology* 4, no. 3 (2015). *https://doi.org/10.1186/s41239-018-0096-z*

Martel, Yann. *Life of Pi: A Novel*. Canada: Knopf Doubleday Publishing Group, 2001.

Mass, Wendy. *Jeremy Fink and the Meaning of Life*. New York: Little Brown & Co, 2008.

May, Kaitlyn and Anastasia Elder. "Efficient, Helpful, or Distracting? A Literature Review of Media Multitasking in Relation to Academic Performance." *International Journal of Educational Technology in Higher Education* 15, no. 13 (2018). *https://doi.org/10.1186/s41239-018-0096-z*

Pandey, Geeta. "Indian Man to Sue Parents for Giving Birth to Him." *BBC News*, February 7, 2019. *https://www.bbc.com/news/world-asia-india-47154287*

GENEROSITY

GRATITUDE

Borovitz, Neal. "The Mitzvah of Gratitude: Parashat Ekev." *World Union for Progressive Judaism*, 2021. *https://wupj.org/library/uncategorized/14443/the-mitzvah-of-gratitude-parashat-ekev/*

DeSteno, David. "Why Gratitude is Wasted on Thanksgiving." *New York Times*, November 23, 2019. *https://www.nytimes.com/interactive/2019/11/23/opinion/sunday/thanksgiving-gratitude.html*

Emmons, Robert and Michael McCullough. *The Psychology of Gratitude*. New York: Oxford University Press, 2004.

Fletcher, Emily. "The Neuroscience of Gratitude." *HuffPost*, November 24, 2015. *https://www.huffpost.com/entry/the-neuroscience-of-gratitude_b_8631392*

Freshwater, Shawna. "Understanding Emotions." *Spacious Therapy*, May 10, 2017. *https://spacioustherapy.com/understanding-emotions/*

Gregoire, Carolyn. "Buddhist Teacher Jack Kornfiled On Gratitude, The Mindful Revolution, And Learning To Embrace Suffering." *HuffPost*, May 5, 2014. *https://www.huffpost.com/entry/buddhist-teacher-jack-kor_n_5249627*

Lesavich, Stephen. "Vibration." *Positive Impact Global*, 2019. *https://positiveimpactempire.com/wp-content/uploads/2019/11/Positive-Impact-Global-Inspiration-Project-Letter-7-V.pdf*

"Modeh Ani: What and Why." *Chabad.org News*, Accessed October 7, 2021. *https://www.chabad.org/library/article_cdo/aid/623937/jewish/Modeh-Ani-What-and-Why.htm*

Peterson, Christopher and Martin Seligman. *Character Strengths and Virtues: A Handbook and Classification*. New York: Oxford University Press, 2004.

Steindl-Rast, David. "Want to be Happy? Be Grateful." Filmed June 2013. TED Video. https://www.ted.com/talks/david_steindl_rast_want_to_be_happy_be_grateful?language=en

Tougar, Eli. "Entering Deeper and Deeper." *Chabad.org News*, Accessed October 7, 2021. https://www.chabad.org/therebbe/article_cdo/aid/82736/jewish/In-the-Garden-of-the-Torah-Savo.htm

APPRECIATION

Chabad.org. "Tzaddik, Rasha & Beionini." *Chabad.org News*. Accessed October 11, 2021. https://www.chabad.org/search/keyword_cdo/kid/2197/jewish/Tzaddik-Rasha-Beinoni.htm

Covey, Stephen R. *The 7 Habits of Highly Effective People: Powerful Lessons in Personal Change.* New York: Simon & Schuster, 2004.

Cramm, Susan. "Do Winners Give—or Take—All?" Strategy+Business. Accessed October 11, 2021. https://www.strategy-business.com/blog/Do-Winners-Give-or-Take-All

Encyclopaedia Britannica Online. Academic ed. s.v. "Karma." Accessed October 7, 2021. https://www.britannica.com/topic/karma.

Grant, Adam. "Are you a Giver or a Taker?" Filmed November 2016. TED Video. https://www.ted.com/talks/adam_grant_are_you_a_giver_or_a_taker?language=en

Jewish Learning Institute. "Tzaddik, Rasha & Beinoni: The Three Personalities According to the Tanya." November 23, 2020. Video, 3:32. *https://www.youtube.com/watch?v=eMHI_CToLfg*

Lindberg, Sara. "What Are the 12 Laws of Karma?" *HealthLine.* Accessed on October 12, 2021. *https://www.healthline.com/health/laws-of-karma*

Lowry, Mark, and Andrew Greer. "The Thin Line Between Priest and Prostitute ft. Becca Stevens and Russ Taff." 2017. In Dinner Conversations. Podcast, MP3 audio. *https://podcasts.apple.com/ca/podcast/thin-line-between-priest-prostitute-ft-becca-stevens/id1290412399?i=1000442489869*

Riess, Helen. "The Science of Empathy." *Journal of Patient Experience* 4, no. 2 (2017). *https://doi.org/10.1177/2374373517699267*

Stanford Encyclopedia of Philosophy. Academic ed. s.v. "Egoism." Accessed October 11, 2021, *https://plato.stanford.edu/entries/egoism/*

Thistle Farms. "National Network." Accessed October 11, 2021. *https://thistlefarms.org/pages/national-network*

Zhan, Lexia, Dingring Guo, Gang Chen, and Joingjoing Yang. "Effects of Repetition Learning on Associative Recognition Over Time: Role of the Hippocampus and Prefrontal Cortex." *Frontiers in Human Neuroscience* 12 (2018) 277. *https://doi.org/10.3389/fnhum.2018.00277*

UNDERSTANDING

Chamberlain Alyssa, Matthew Gricius, Danielle Wallace, Diana Borjas, and Vincent Ware. "Parolee-Parole Officer Rapport: Does It Impact Recidivism?" *International Journal of Offender Therapy and Comparative Criminology* 62, no. 11 (2018). https://doi.org/10.1177/0306624X17741593

Fredrickson, Barbara L. "What Good Are Positive Emotions?" *Review of General Psychology: Journal of Division 1, of the American Psychological Association* 2, no. 3 (1998). https://doi.org/10.1037/1089-2680.2.3.300

Fredrickson, Barbara, Michael Cohn, Kimberly Coffey, Jolynn Pek, and Sandra Finkel. "Open Hearts Build Lives: Positive Emotions, Induced through Loving-kindness Meditation, Build Consequential Personal Resources." *Journal of Personality and Social Psychology*, 95, no. 5 (2008). https://doi.org/10.1037/a0013262

Gillett, Rachel. "5 Reasons Google is the Best Place to Work in America and No Other Company Can Touch It." *Business Insider*. April 28, 2016. https://www.businessinsider.com/google-is-the-best-company-to-work-for-in-america-2016-4

Hechter, Michael and Satoshi Kanazawa. "Sociological Rational Choice Theory." *Annual Review of Sociology* 23 (1997). https://doi.org/10.1146/annurev.soc.23.1.191

Lei, Hao, Yunhuo Cui, and Chiu Ming Ming. "The Relationship between Teacher Support and Students' Academic Emotions: A Meta-Analysis." *Frontiers in Psychology*. 8 (2018). https://doi.org/10.3389/fpsyg.2017.02288

Owens, Bradley, Michael Johnson, and Terence Michael. "Expressed Humility in Organizations: Implications for Performance, Teams, and Leadership." *Organization Science* 24, no. 5 (2013). https://doi.org/10.1287/orsc.1120.0795

Ozbay, Fatih, Douglas Johnson, Eleni Dimoulas, C. A. Morgan, Dennis Charney, and Steven Southwick. "Social Support and Resilience to Stress: From Neurobiology to Clinical Practice." *Psychiatry* 4, no. 5 (2007). https://www.ncbi.nlm.nih.gov/pmc/articles/PMC2921311/

Sheng, Ellen. "Why the Headquarters of Iconic Tech Companies are Now Among America's Top Tourist Attractions." *CNBC*, December 3, 2018. https://www.cnbc.com/2018/11/03/why-the-headquarters-of-iconic-tech-companies-are-tourist-attractions.html

Valiente, Carlos, Jodi Swanson, and Nancy Eisenberg. "Linking Students' Emotions and Academic Achievement: When and Why Emotions Matter." *Child Development Perspectives.* 6, no. 2 (2012). https://doi.org/10.1111/j.1750-8606.2011.00192.x

Yang, JianChun, Wei Zhang, and Xiao Chen. "Why Do Leaders Express Humility and How Does This Matter: A Rational Choice Perspective." *Frontiers in Psychology* 10 (2019). https://doi.org/10.3389/fpsyg.2019.01925Courage

COURAGE

TAKE RISKS

Banayan, Alex. *The Third Door: The Wild Quest to Uncover How the World's Most Successful People Launched Their Careers.* New York: Crown Publishing Group, 2018.

BBC Northern Ireland Learning. "Buddhism." Teacher's Notes. Accessed October 14, 2021. https://www.bbc.co.uk/northernireland/schools/11_16/citizenship/pdfs/ctz_rel_pg01_tn02.pdf

Desmarais, Christina. "Why Risk Takers Do Better in Business and in Life: Playing it Safe Often isn't in your Best Interest. Here's Why." *Inc.*, October 10, 2014. https://www.inc.com/christina-desmarais/why-risk-takers-do-better-in-business-and-life.html

Golstein, Kurt. *The Organism*. New York: Zone Books, 2000.

Pickersgill, Martyn, Paul Martin, and Sarah Cunningham-Burley. "The Changing Brain: Neuroscience and the Enduring Import of Everyday Experience." Public Understanding of Science 24, no. 7 (2015). https://doi.org/10.1177/0963662514521550

Rhimes, Shonda. *Year of Yes: How to Dance It Out, Stand In the Sun and Be Your Own Person.* New York: Simon & Schuster, 2016.

Ruisi, Chris. "Complacency: The Silent Business Killer." *American Express*. September 11, 2017. https://www.americanexpress.com/en-us/business/trends-and-insights/articles/complacency-silent-business-killer/

Torben, Rick. "Killed by a Corporate Culture of Complacency." *Corporate Culture* (blog). February 11, 2015. https://www.torbenrick.eu/blog/culture/killed-by-a-corporate-culture-of-complacency/

Troianovski, Anton and Sven Grundberg. "Nokia's Bad Call on Smartphones." *Wall Street Journal*, July 18, 2012. https://www.wsj.com/articles/SB10001424052702304388004577531002591315494

NEVER ASSUME

Morin, Amy. "The Secret of Becoming Mentally Strong" Filmed December 2015. TED Video. https://www.youtube.com/watch?v=TFbv757kup4

AUTHENTICITY

PURPOSEFUL THINKING

Choi, Catherine. "New Year's Resolution Statistics." *Finder* (blog). Updated Dec 4, 2020. https://www.finder.com/new-years-resolution-statistics

Committee on Department of Homeland Security Occupational Health and Operational Medicine Infrastructure; Board on Health Sciences Policy; Institute of Medicine. Advancing Workforce Health at the Department of Homeland Security: Protecting Those Who Protect Us. "Organizational

Alignment and Coordination." Washington (DC): National Academies Press, (2014): 6. https://www.ncbi.nlm.nih.gov/books/NBK231899/

Garvin, David A., and Joshua Margolis. "The Art of Giving and Receiving Advice." *Harvard Business Review*, January–February 2015. https://hbr.org/2015/01/the-art-of-giving-and-receiving-advice

Geronimi, Clyde, Hamilton Luske, and Wilfred Jackson, dirs. *Cinderella*. 1950; Burbank, CA: Walt Disney Productions. 2005. DVD.

Gollwitzer, Peter M. and Robert Wicklund. *Symbolic Self-completion*. New York: Psychology Press, 1982.

Schippers, Michaela C. and Niklas Ziegler. "Life Crafting as a Way to Find Purpose and Meaning in Life." *Frontiers in Psychology* 10, 2018. https://doi.org/10.3389/fpsyg.2019.02778

Sivers, Derek. "Keep Your Goals to Yourself." Filmed 2010. TED Video. https://www.ted.com/talks/derek_sivers_keep_your_goals_to_yourself/transcript?language=en#:~:text=The%20repeated%20psychology%20tests%20have,d%20actually%20done%20the%20work

Velasco, Ferran, Joan Manuel Batista-Foguet, and Robert Emmerling. "Are We Making Progress? Assessing Goal-Directed Behaviors in Leadership Development Programs." *Frontiers in Psychology*, 10 (2019). https://doi.org/10.3389/fpsyg.2019.01345

THINK BIG AND IDENTIFY YOUR TRUE WHY

Becker, Joshua. "What is Minimalism?" *Becoming Minimalist.* Accessed October 11, 2021. https://www.becomingminimalist.com/what-is-minimalism/

D'Avella, Matt, dir. *The Minimalists: Less is Now.* 2021; Los Angeles, CA: Booklight Productions and Catalyst Films. Netflix.

John, Peter Newton. "Former Harvard Admissions Interviewer Shares 5 Questions she Asked Almost Every Applicant." *LinkedIn Pulse,* November 2, 2016. https://www.linkedin.com/pulse/former-harvard-admissions-interviewer-shares-5-she-peter-newton-john/

Ryan, R.M. and E.L. Deci. "On Happiness and Human Potentials: A Review of Research on Hedonic and Eudaimonic Well-being." *Annual Review in Psychology.* 52 (2001). https://doi.org/10.1146/annurev.psych.52.1.141.

Steger, Michael, Shigehiro Oishi, and Todd Kashdan. "Meaning in Life Across the Life Span: Levels and Correlates of Meaning in Life from Emerging Adulthood to Older Adulthood." *Journal of Positive Psychology* 4, no. 1 (2009). https://doi.org/10.1080/17439760802303127

Suh, Hanna, Philip B. Gnilka, and Kenneth Rice. "Perfectionism and Well-being: A Positive Psychology Framework." *Personality and Individual Differences* 111, no. 1 (2017). https://doi.org/10.1016/j.paid.2017.01.041

Thioux, Marc, Valeria Gazzola, and Christian Keysers. "Action Understanding: How, What and Why." *Current Biology* 18, no. 10 (2008). https://doi.org/10.1016/j.cub.2008.03.018

VISUALIZE YOUR "WHY" IN ACTION

Alshogre, Omar. "What I Learned In Prison" Filmed April 2019. TED Video. https://www.ted.com/talks/omar_alshogre_what_i_learned_in_prison

Arlinghaus, Katherine R., and Craig Johnston. "The Importance of Creating Habits and Routine." *American Journal of Lifestyle Medicine* 13. no. 2 (2019). https://doi.org/10.1177/1559827618818044

Clarey, Christopher. "Olympians Use Imagery as Mental Training." *New York Times*, February 23, 2014. https://www.nytimes.com/2014/02/23/sports/olympics/olympians-use-imagery-as-mental-training.html

Cleere, Michelle. "Mental Moment: Psychoneuromuscular Theory." *Dr. Michelle* (blog). June 19, 2012. https://drmichellecleere.com/blog/mental-moment-psychoneuromuscular-theory/

Shukla, Aditya. "The Scientific Truth Behind Fake It Till You Make it." *Cognition Today*. Updated December 9, 2020. https://cognitiontoday.com/the-scientific-truth-behind-fake-it-till-you-make-it/

ALIGN YOUR HOW TO CREATE SYNERGY

Bahrami, Susan, Saeed Rajaeepour, Hasan Rizi, Monereh Zahmatkesh, and Zahra Nematolahi. "The Relationship Between Students' Study Habits, Happiness and Depression." *Iranian Journal of Nursing and Midwifery Research*, 16, no. 3 (2011). https://www.ncbi.nlm.nih.gov/pmc/articles/PMC3249802/

Bryant, Sean. "How Many Startups Fail and Why?" *Investopedia*, November 9, 2020. https://www.investopedia.com/articles/personal-finance/040915/how-many-startups-fail-and-why.asp

Bureau of Labor Statistics. "Number of Jobs, Labor Market Experience, Marital Status, and Health: Results from a National Longitudinal Survey." US Department of Labor. August 13, 2021. https://www.bls.gov/news.release/pdf/nlsoy.pdf

Burley, Todd. "A Phenomenologically Based Theory of Personality." *Penn State University Press* 16, no. 1 (2012). https://doi.org/10.5325/gestaltreview.16.1.0007.

Foster, Sarah. "Survey: 55% of Americans Expect to Search for a New Job Over the Next 12 Months." *Bankrate Personal Finance* (blog). August 23, 2021. https://www.bankrate.com/personal-finance/job-seekers-survey-august-2021/

Gardner, Benjamin, Phillippa Lally, and Jane Wardle. "Making Health Habitual: The Psychology of 'Habit-formation' and General Practice." *British Journal of General Practice* 62, no. 605 (2012). https://doi.org/10.3399/bjgp12X659466

Pew Research Center. *The State of American Jobs.* October, 2016. https://www.pewresearch.org/social-trends/wp-content/uploads/sites/3/2016/10/ST_2016.10.06_Future-of-Work_FINAL4-1.pdf.

www.ingramcontent.com/pod-product-compliance
Lightning Source LLC
LaVergne TN
LVHW011812060526
838200LV00053B/3751